Dual-handed nonprofit leadership approach.

Edward N. Joiner

Abstract

Models of leadership effectiveness have evolved over time as the understanding of leadership has changed. Ambidextrous leadership is defined as the simultaneous use of exploration and exploitation to pursue a balance of innovation and production. This balance can occur through shared leadership or through the ambidextrous nature of individual leaders adapting to environmental variables. While ambidexterity has been studied in many different contexts, the nonprofit sector has explored this subject in a limited way. Nonprofit organizations use shared leadership models and are required to frequently adapt to new environments due to fiscal and organizational capacity challenges. The purpose of this qualitative study was to understand the skills and knowledge that nonprofit leaders utilize to implement ambidextrous leadership practices within their respective organizations. Information gained through individual interviews with nonprofit leaders was analyzed using a grounded theory approach. Findings indicated that joint space through collaboration and the use of shared leadership was a key driver in the pursuit of both innovation and productivity. Leaders engage in a dynamic cycle of behaviors contingent on multiple situational factors. This proposed model adds further detail on the stages involved in the innovation and production processes, while clarifying the barriers and contingencies involved from the perspective of nonprofit leaders. Elements of the conceptual framework should be considered by nonprofit leaders when engaging in strategic planning. Additionally, the study provides a deeper understanding regarding the unique needs of nonprofit organizations in their resource management and human resource management. Finally, this research adds to the scholarship around ambidextrous leadership as it applies to nonprofit contexts.

Table of Contents

List of Tables

List of Figures

Chapter 1: Nature of the Study

Background

The nonprofit sector plays an important role in our country's economic landscape, contributing to 5% of the gross domestic product (GDP) of the United States (NCCS, 2020). Nonprofit organizations are often seen as a bridge, operating in collaboration with both the private sector and government entities (Shier & Handy, 2020). Nonprofits provide entry points for citizens to engage in their communities, either on a paid or volunteer basis (Mathews, 2020). In addition to serving as the third largest employer, an estimated 64 million adults (or 25% of the population) volunteered at least once in the last year for a nonprofit organization (NCCS, 2020).

The nonprofit sector is diverse, ranging from small entities with a working board of directors and a limited cohort of paid employees managing operations to large, multi-million-dollar organizations that operate multiple programs and have a complex matrix structure (NCCS, 2020). While all organizations must consider their structure and staffing with respect to capacity, nonprofit organizations face additional challenges in often being forced to *do more with less* or operate within a starvation cycle (Gregory & Howard, 2009). Organizational resilience for nonprofit organizations, found chiefly in their ability to adapt to circumstances, is important for sustainability (Shier & Handy, 2020; Witmer & Mellinger, 2016).

Because of these needs, it is incumbent on nonprofit leaders to develop a keen awareness of their organization's capacity and the particular skills or strategies that will support opportunities to maximize their organization's mission and vision using their current capabilities (Peng, 2019). Leadership within nonprofit organizations can be complex due to many factors (Gilstrap et al., 2016). It is often not easily explained through one mechanism or style but is dependent on situational factors and skills (Yukl, 2012). Within complex models, leadership is present at multiple levels of an organization and different skills may be needed based on role or placement within the organizational hierarchy (Bish & Becker, 2016; Schulze & Pinkow, 2020; Yukl, 2012).

It is important for nonprofit leaders to develop a broad understanding of leadership that is rooted in complex systems and human resources management (Uhl-Bien & Arena, 2018). Use of an ambidextrous approach to organizational management supports the balance of simultaneously driving innovation while maintaining efficiency within existing resources (Sun et al., 2020). While these models have been studied in the for-profit business context, studies within the nonprofit sector are more limited (Bouwmans et al., 2019; Gerlach et al., 2020; Havermans et al., 2015).

A grounded theory approach to the role of ambidextrous leadership in the nonprofit sector supports a generative approach to the topic (Corbin & Strauss, 2015). Previous research has used a case study approach or looked at ambidexterity within a very limited organizational scope of the sector (Gilstrap et al., 2016; Peng, 2019; Witmer & Mellinger, 2016). A grounded theory approach also supports the role that equifinality plays in understanding the diverse needs of the nonprofit sector and the possibility of a combination of solutions for resilient organizational management (Cannaerts et al., 2020).

Problem Statement

The nonprofit sector accounts for 10% of the U.S. workforce and is the 3rd largest employer (NCCS, 2020). As nonprofit organizations are increasingly called to develop a business focus, questions arise as to whether the skill set of nonprofit leaders should be different from those in the for-profit workforce (Bish & Becker, 2016). Market forces and a continual struggle for resources call for nonprofit organizations to also deliver programs in socially

innovative ways (Shier & Handy, 2020).

Nonprofit organizations constantly face challenges in building capacity, finding

themselves stretched to the limit for resources while also placing priority on program delivery

(Zhang et al., 2017). They must continually balance their need to innovate and their need to

produce (Gibson & Birkinshaw, 2004; Uhl-Bien & Arena, 2018). The interplay of nonprofit

leaders with internal and external stakeholders is key to organizational success (Mathews, 2020;

Mulenga et al., 2018; Shier & Handy, 2016). Other factors, such as the organization's position

within its life cycle and situational crises influence leadership decisions and organizational

choices (Dóci et al., 2020; Rojas, 2018). However, leadership styles and capabilities for

individuals in the nonprofit sector have not been investigated with the same rigor as those in the

for-profit sector (Aboramadan & Kundi, 2020; Bish & Becker, 2016; Brimhall, 2021).

The transformational leadership style is frequently cited as an effective tool for

implementing strategic changes or building a strong nonprofit organization (Mary, 2005; Valero

et al., 2015). However, it is actually the use of an ambidextrous style that leads to the most

sustainable outcomes (Bouwmans et al., 2019; Severgnini et al., 2019; Uhl-Bien & Arena, 2018).

Ambidextrous leaders utilize a combination of behaviors in different contexts to achieve a

balance between innovation and production, which can include collaborative efforts between

leaders who engage in different behaviors based on situational factors.

The general organizational leadership problem is that when nonprofit organizations do

not assess their innovation and production needs based on identifiable criteria, this decreases the

capacity of the organization to fulfill its mission. The specific organizational leadership problem

is that nonprofit leaders may not always identify key moments and practices in which particular path of ambidextrous leadership would be most impactful (to innovation or production). This study will contribute to the body of knowledge needed to address this problem by examining the use of an ambidextrous approach by leaders working in nonprofit contexts.

Purpose of the Study

The purpose of this qualitative grounded theory study was to understand the skills and knowledge that nonprofit leaders utilize to implement ambidextrous leadership practices within their respective organizations. Ambidextrous leadership is generally defined as a flexible response to situational factors in order to facilitate maximal opportunities within the organization for innovation or production (Sun et al., 2020). As nonprofit leaders are called to balance current capacity with the need to drive their mission, the use of ambidextrous leadership is vital to success (Zhang et al., 2017). These practices may be utilized through a shared leadership model within the organization or in collaboration and partnership with other community organizations.

Research Questions

The primary research question under investigation for this study was: how do nonprofit leaders use ambidextrous leadership practices to support their organization's unique needs for innovation and production?

The following subquestions were also addressed:

1. How do nonprofit leaders use elements of ambidextrous leadership to collaborate with other organizations or utilize a shared leadership model?

2. What elements of ambidextrous leadership are most supportive to a nonprofit organization's need for innovation?

3. What elements of ambidextrous leadership are most supportive to a nonprofit organization's need for production?

Conceptual Framework

Glaser (1978) posited that a grounded theory research design can use a variety of models to set the framework for a theoretical coding approach to a research question. Using one of these approaches can help the researcher utilize the data collected to generate theory. This empirical design pulls from a positivist epistemology. One model in particular, the Six C's, serves as a foundational base for grounded theory research. It considers the relationship between Causes, Contexts, Contingencies, Consequences, Covariances, and Conditions (see Figure 1).

Figure 1

The Six C's Model

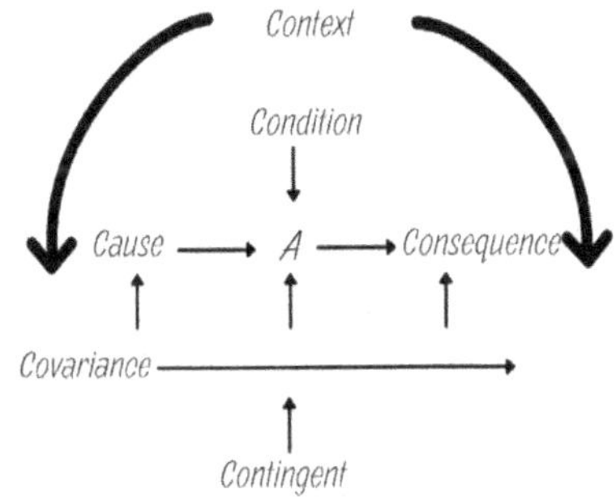

From Glaser (1978)

Using Glaser's Six C's model as a starting point, I created a conceptual framework that supported the exploration of my research questions. The <u>context</u> for the framework started with a grounded theory approach that combined my prior experience with exploration of the processes present within the phenomenon under investigation (Charmaz, 2014). A grounded theory approach also supported a pragmatic epistemology that grounded the pursuit of solutions to situations encountered by practitioners in the working world (Creswell & Poth, 2018).

Nonprofit organizations continually assess their performance and effectiveness along a growing continuum with respect to their programs, management, governance, financial resources, and systems. In this framework, two factors set the conditions for this work. The first is the organization's place in the lifecycle (Rojas, 2018). The second is the direction and implementation of the organization's overall strategy (use of organizational ambidexterity) (Sun et al., 2020). Further, an organization's position within the life cycle helps to define the role of the leadership (board of directors and/or paid leadership) (Mathews, 2020).

Nonprofit organizations must continually balance their need to innovate and their need to produce (Uhl-Bien & Arena, 2018). This organizational ambidexterity often functions hand-in-hand with the organization's position within its life cycle (Gibson & Birkinshaw, 2004). For example, a new organization or one experiencing significant growth will have different innovation/production needs than an organization that is mature and stable (Kenny-Stevens, 2008; Uhl-Bien & Arena, 2018).

Situational factors such as crises, time pressure, and risk exert influence on leaders as a covariance. These factors influence leadership behavior in the accomplishment of these aims (Fazzi & Zamaro, 2016; Gilstrap et al., 2016; Judge & Piccolo, 2004). Another element of covariance includes collaborators, competitors, and the current community need (Bolden et al., 2020; Shier & Handy, 2020; Witmer & Mellinger, 2016).

The behavior under investigation was how leaders of nonprofit organizations utilize their individual ambidexterity to determine the skills and capabilities needed to accomplish the organization's aims (consequences) effectively. Previous research on ambidextrous leadership in other settings tells us that the use of exploration (opening) behaviors will lead to innovation and the use of exploitation (closing) behaviors will lead to production or efficiency (Gerlach et al., 2020; Uhl-Bien & Arena, 2018). This may include accomplishment of the organization's mission and vision, completion of strategic outcomes, or effective use of funding.

What is less clear are the specific leadership behaviors (opening and closing behaviors) of nonprofit leaders that lead to innovation and production outcomes (Peng, 2019; Witmer & Mellinger, 2016). Further, the role that collaboration plays in supporting these outcomes was also under investigation (Mathews, 2020; Shier & Handy, 2020). The aim of this dissertation was to understand how nonprofit leaders determine how and when they should use particular skills and tools to support their organization's unique needs in accomplishing their organizational aims. See Figure 2 for a visual representation of this conceptual framework.

Figure 2

Visual Representation of the Conceptual Framework

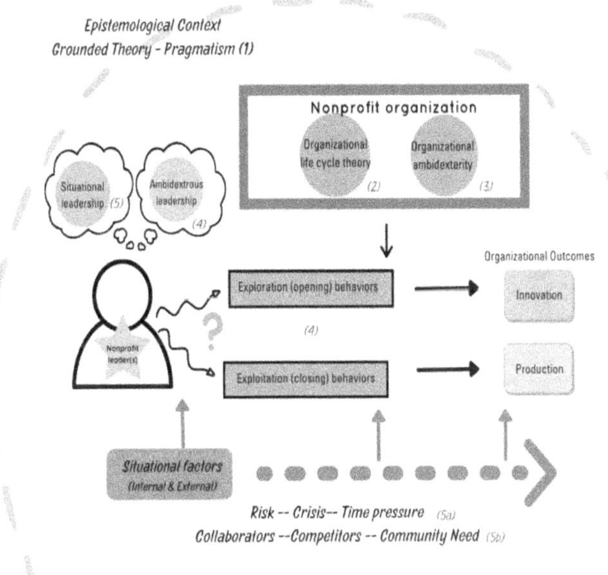

Research supporting the conceptual framework:
1. Charmaz, 2014; Creswell & Poth, 2018; Glaser, 1978;
2. Gibson & Birkenshaw, 2004; Mathews, 2020; Rojas, 2018; Uhl-Bien & Arena, 2018
3. Sun et al., 2020; Uhl-Bien & Arena, 2018
4. Gerlach et al., 2020; Mathews, 2020, Peng, 2018; Shier & Handy, 2020; Witmer & Mellinger, 2016
5a. Fazzi & Zamaro, 2016; Gilstrap et al., 2016; Judge & Piccolo, 2004
5b. Bolden et al., 2020; Shier & Handy, 2020; Witmer & Mellinger, 2016

Scope of the Study

The scope of inquiry was limited to individuals with at least 3 years of experience in the nonprofit sector. Leadership was defined to include both executive level and mid-level or unit-level roles within their respective organization. Leadership experience was also defined as having fiscal, administrative, and programmatic responsibility for their organization, whether overall or within a particular division. Three years of experience was relevant for the study as subjects would have perspective within their organizational role both before and during the COVID-19 pandemic.

This study also focused on nonprofit organizations that had annual budgets of at least $500,000. Even though 88% of nonprofit organizations have an annual budget of less than $500,000 (National Council of Nonprofits, 2019), organizations smaller than this size would be less likely to have full-time staff or the capacity to speak to the research questions under investigation. Primary geographic outreach for the study was the Richmond, Virginia area. This was an area accessible to me that included over 1,740 nonprofit organizations of varying sizes and structures (Community Foundation for a Greater Richmond, 2021) and allowed for greater access to subjects for in-person interviews. However, recruitment criteria was not limited based on geography and nonprofit leaders who otherwise qualified were included.

Definitions of Key Terms

Ambidexterity. Responding to situational needs of an organization or program using a flexible approach or style (Sun et al., 2020).

Ambidextrous leadership. A leadership style characterized by the use of complementary behaviors to elicit innovation or efficiency from teams when most appropriate to the situational needs of the organization, team, or project (Zacher & Rosing, 2015).

Complexity leadership (theory). A leadership theory that acknowledges the multi-faceted nature of organizations that function to produce knowledge in a continually adaptive space (Uhl-Bien & Arena, 2018). Complex systems utilize a combination of entrepreneurial, operational, and enabling leadership. These styles may be elicited by singular leaders in different capacities over time or within a collaborative, shared leadership model.

Entrepreneurial leadership. Entrepreneurial leadership allows for changes in reaction to events. It utilizes a situational approach to decision making. Entrepreneurial leadership embraces comfort with tension and encourages creativity in driving solutions (Uhl-Bien & Arena, 2018). Previous iterations of the model called this adaptive leadership (Uhl-Bien et al., 2007).

Operational leadership. Operational leadership provides structure to the organization. It provides rules, direction, constraints, and demands within the system (Uhl-Bien & Arena, 2018). Previous iterations of the model called this administrative leadership (Uhl-Bien et al., 2007).

Enabling leadership. Enabling leadership often sits between administrative and adaptive leadership to stimulate balance between the other functions. Enabling leadership supports flexibility within the system, allowing for bending and movement within the structure that administrative leadership provides while reinforcing the creativity and tension that arise from adaptive leadership (Uhl-Bien et al., 2007).

Exploitation (closing) behaviors. Work behaviors characterized by adherence to rules and structure, aligned with efficiency and productivity (Junni et al., 2013; Zacher & Rosing, 2015).

Exploration (opening) behaviors. Work behaviors characterized by innovation, ingenuity, and transformational change (Junni et al., 2013; Zacher & Rosing, 2015).

Innovation. A business process that involves the generation of new ideas followed by the successful implementation of these ideas (Rosing & Zacher, 2017).

Nonprofit organization. An organization whose mission is to serve the public good, rather than make a profit. Nonprofit organizations within the United States are registered and certified by the Internal Revenue Service (IRS) as public charities under IRS tax code 501(c)3 (other than private foundations) and governed by a board of directors (NCCS, 2020).

Organizational ambidexterity. The use of tension and flexibility within an organization in order to secure balanced solutions for programmatic needs (Peng, 2019). Organizational ambidexterity can be structural, decisional, or hierarchical (Peng, 2019; Sun et al., 2020).

Organizational capacity. The capability of an organization to respond to its changing needs, either through funding, staffing, or structural adaptation (Zhang et al., 2017).

Situational leadership (theory). An adaptive leadership style characterized by adjusting within teams, projects or organizations based on the internal or external needs of the organization (Uhl-Bien et al., 2007; Yukl, 2012).

Taxonomy of leadership behavior (Yukl). A theory of leadership in which leader actions are defined in terms of broad categories of relations-oriented and task-oriented behaviors, often elicited based on situational variables (Yukl et al., 2002).

Transformational leadership. A leadership style that is used to describe people who are visionary, motivational, and inductive (Burke, 2018)

Transactional leadership. A leadership style that is used to describe people who typically excel at tasks that are administrative in nature and utilize short-term or deductive thinking (Burke, 2018).

Significance of the Study

As nonprofit organizations seek to maximize resources and opportunities, it is important to understand the role that leaders at all levels can play to support an ambidextrous framework.

Most nonprofit organizations are relatively small with 88% carrying an annual budget of less than $500,000 (National Council of Nonprofits, 2019). Nonprofits, however, do not solely rely on charitable giving for their sustainability. In fact, almost 80% of nonprofit revenue is a result of fees for program services, government contracts, and grants tied to specific program deliverables (National Council of Nonprofits, 2019). With most nonprofit organizations operating with less than 1 month of reserves, it is imperative that nonprofit organizations seek leadership that can think nimbly and strategically over the course of economic crises, community changes, and market fluctuations.

Results of this study inform nonprofit leaders and boards when considering staffing needs. Finding a leader (or set of leaders) who can utilize an ambidextrous approach to directing strategy and program needs is crucial to an organization's success (Bish & Becker, 2016; Mary, 2005; Routhieaux, 2015). The results of this study will also support nonprofit organizations in maximizing their existing resources, particularly when engaging in collaborative efforts with similarly aligned groups (Koster & van Bree, 2018; Shier & Handy, 2020). A 2021 survey of nonprofit organizations in Virginia found that almost 90% of respondents engage in collaborative work with other organizations, usually through joint programming or information sharing (CNE, 2021).

Finally, the study will provide a deeper understanding regarding the unique needs of nonprofit organizations in their resource management and human resource management. While research on these topics within the nonprofit sector is growing, it is still an acknowledged gap that requires further exploration (Aboramadan & Kundi, 2020; Brimhall, 2021).

Summary

Nonprofit organizations play an important role in our economy and community (NCCS, 2020). With an implied mandate to do more with less, nonprofit organizations must constantly prioritize their needs and resources in order to remain resilient (Shier & Handy, 2020; Witmer & Mellinger, 2016). Nonprofit leaders can use an ambidextrous approach that simultaneously drives innovation while balancing existing resources (Sun et al., 2020). This approach is used frequently in organizations that must balance complex needs and collaborative sharing of resources and information (Uhl-Bien et al., 2007). However, it is unclear how nonprofit leaders currently use these approaches in their work. A grounded theory approach supports an inductive understanding of the way nonprofit leaders utilize ambidextrous practices to balance their organization's needs for innovation and production.

Chapter 2 of this dissertation will provide background on the theoretical understanding of ambidextrous and complex leadership within the context of organizational leadership theories over the last century. Rationale for the movement towards a taxonomy approach and a situational approach to leadership behavior will also be shared. Research on the use of ambidexterity and situational leadership in for-profit business contexts will be shared. The literature review will also cover what makes the leadership needs of the nonprofit sector unique as well as the limited research and inherent gap that remains to be explored on the use of ambidexterity within the nonprofit sector.

Chapter 3 of this dissertation will explain why a grounded theory approach was the most conducive to the study of the research questions under exploration. Design and methodology for the study, including instrumentation and data processing procedures will be described. Ethical considerations, considerations for validity, assumptions, and limitations inherent to the study are

also included.

Chapter 4 describes the results collected from the coding and analysis of individual

semistructured interviews that were conducted with nonprofit leaders. Insights regarding answers

to the core research questions are shared as well as additional information gained through

conversations with research participants. Chapter 5 delves into the analysis that emerged from

this research study. Limitations, implications for further research, and recommendations for

practitioners are shared.

Chapter 2: Literature Review

Introduction

This literature review provides an overview of perspectives in leadership effectiveness from the latter part of the 20th century into current theories that include complexity and ambidexterity. This review covers an overview of theories related to leadership style and effectiveness with the emergence of complexity leadership and ambidextrous leadership as recent theoretical frameworks for understanding organizational needs. Current research exploring the characteristics and effectiveness of ambidextrous leadership in multiple settings is shared. Finally, the specific organizational needs within the nonprofit sector and specific leadership research within this sector provide additional context for the research gap that is under investigation. While there is a great deal of research on ambidextrous leadership in for-profit contexts, the nonprofit sector has not received the same degree of attention. Much of the research that has examined shared leadership or use of situational styles in the nonprofit sector has been done in limited contexts or from other theoretical frameworks besides ambidexterity.

Research Strategy

In order to conduct this literature review, a variety of sources were utilized. Searches were conducted via Google Scholar, ProQuest, and EBSCO Host. The following search terms were used (in varying combinations) to narrow results: transformational leadership, leadership styles, nonprofit/not-for-profit, augmentation effect, ambidexterity, organizational ambidexterity, ambidextrous leadership, complexity leadership, nonprofit leadership, innovation, situational leadership, Yukl taxonomy, exploration and exploitation, enabling leadership, and qualitative. Results from the last 5 years (2016-2021) were prioritized. Combined searches resulted in over

460 results. Additionally, textbooks and reference tools from the author's private library were utilized as resources.

Early Perspectives on Leadership Effectiveness

Stemming from the Industrial Revolution, early examinations of leadership effectiveness in the 20th century were rooted in manufacturing and other manual labor technologies (Sashkin & Burke, 1990). This research focused its energy on supervision and management. It wasn't until the latter part of the 20th century that leadership research generally shifted its attention to look at the behavior of leaders at higher organizational levels.

In fact, differentiations between roles of leadership and management continue into the 21st century. Burke (2018) makes distinctions between the roles of leaders and managers, painting leaders as people who are *visionary, motivational,* and *inductive* while managers are described in terms of *administrative, short-term thinking,* and *deductive.* Instead of thinking of managers and leaders as separate and distinct roles within an organization, however, others assert that leadership is embedded in the work of (and practiced by) those who effectively manage (Mintzberg, 2009). Ford (2016) further clarifies that leadership is a relatively fluid concept that should not be examined from a single, static dimension. The general conclusion drawn by the modern understanding of effective organizational leadership is that it is shaped by a combination of (a) the personal characteristics of leaders (b) the organizational contexts in which they act and (c) specific actions which the leaders take (Burke, 2018; Ford, 2016; Mintzberg, 2009; Sashkin & Burke, 1990).

The Transformational–Transactional Leadership Dyad

As the study of leadership effectiveness evolved in the 1970s and 80s, the transformational and transactional leadership dyad became a dominant paradigm for understanding leadership styles. With this model, the behavior (actions) of leaders are seen as a function of the person and the situation interacting together (Sashkin & Burke, 1990). As they utilize their individual styles, leaders take on specific roles. This, in turn, directs the organization and shapes the culture.

Transformational leaders reflect visionary thinking and are often characterized as *charismatic, revolutionary,* and *mission driven.* Contrastingly, transactional leaders tend to focus on *refinement, task-orientation,* and *short-term tasks.* In this way, those exhibiting transformational styles are seen as *leaders* while transactional styles are ascribed to *managers* (Burke, 2018). The transformational leadership style is frequently cited as an effective tool for implementing strategic changes or building a strong organization (Mary, 2005; Valero et al., 2015). However, a large meta-analysis lends support to the validity of both styles used in a leadership context (Judge & Piccolo, 2004). This research supports an augmentation effect with the use of styles contingent to particular situations.

Despite prior research seeking to delineate and discriminate the effectiveness of one style over another, more recent research indicates that transformational and transactional leadership skills are utilized by leaders in tandem and that they mutually strengthen each other (Fazzi & Zamaro, 2016; Judge & Piccolo, 2004). In a large qualitative case study with 42 participants, Mulenga et al. (2018) reflected on the manner in which leadership styles impacted follower perceptions. The researchers identified that both transformational and transactional styles were used by leaders in healthcare to influence followers; however, the conceptual framework of the study was weak. While the interviews with hospital employees identified positive and negative leadership practices that impacted access, quality of care, and hospital responsiveness, the conceptual framework did not clearly identify or describe particular leadership behaviors or characteristics that led to specific outcomes in transformational or transactional categories. Instead, the conceptual framework was shared in very broad or vague terms. Given that the role of a conceptual framework is to provide clarity with the relationship between theoretical constructs and a refined definition of concepts within a problem, this was a distinct weakness in the study (Grant & Osanloo, 2015).

Vecchio et al. (2008) similarly explored the incorporation of elements of both the transformational and transactional leadership styles through a study of 179 teacher–principal dyads in California high schools. Their findings indicated that the use of transformational leadership skills augments a leader's use of transactional leadership skills. This, in turn, enhances employee performance and satisfaction. An important underlying conclusion is that while the transformational style is often prioritized in leadership training, the role of the transactional style is also important and should not be minimized.

Criticisms of the Transformational Style

In the 1990s, new thoughts emerged around leadership style and effectiveness. Yukl (1999) identified criticisms with the transformational and charismatic leadership paradigms. One primary criticism was that the emphasis within these paradigms on emotion and values missed the mark in capturing the specific leadership behaviors that make someone effective or ineffective in their role. Previous research on leader effectiveness typically used factor analysis to analyze specific behavior responses in questionnaires; however, Yukl pointed out that preconceptions about leadership can influence these outcomes (Yukl, 2012). Respondents often have a bias towards a certain archetypal ideal regarding leadership behavior and this bias may skew their perspective. Additionally, factor analysis is less useful when there are multiple paths for achieving a particular aim. Survey responses may be limited to what was observed as opposed to what might be possible (Yukl, 2012). Yukl's criticisms were echoed in later research, citing a combination of lack of rigor in observation and confirmation bias leading to misinterpretation of causal factors that predict effective leadership behaviors (Behrendt et al., 2017).

Additional criticisms of the transformational–transactional dyad emerged from Yukl's research. One is that transactional leadership is often portrayed as a negative characteristic, or it is only positive when used in combination with a transformational style (Yukl, 1999). Another critique is that transformational leadership is biased to favor some stakeholders over others. For example, the transformational style may be perceived as "effective" by owners and customers of the organization but not necessarily by the employees themselves (Yukl, 1999).

There is strong evidence for the effectiveness of the transformational style in demonstrating leadership (Mary, 2005; Valero et al., 2015; Vecchio et al., 2008). Of note is Judge and Piccolo's metanalysis (2004) which examined 87 studies, assessing the validity of the transformational and transactional leadership styles over time and across researchers. However, an important conclusion from the Judge and Piccolo metanalysis is that transformational leadership adds to the effect or use of transactional leadership. Utilizing elements of both leadership styles enhances outcomes and the "best leaders are both transformational and transactional" (Judge & Piccolo, 2004, p. 755).

A main challenge with the transformational/transactional style dyad is that it is unclear what the underlying processes of leader behavior are that directly impact followers (Yukl, 1999). In Yukl's view, transformational leadership emphasized the impact of leaders on individual followers rather than the impact on a group or whole organizational outcomes. The theories that bolster transformational leadership assume that processes are the same in all situations; however,

Yukl noticed that research examining usage of this style rarely (if ever) identified situations where the transformational style might be detrimental (Yukl, 1999, 2012). In their view, many studies examined the quantity of certain leadership behaviors rather than the timing or appropriate use of those behaviors (Yukl, 2012).

Yukl's Taxonomy: Another Perspective

By contrast, Yukl saw leadership tasks in terms of observable behaviors rather than character traits (Yukl et al., 2002). They initially broke down these behaviors into three main categories: task-oriented, relations-oriented, and change oriented; later research added an additional category (external oriented; Yukl, 2012; see Table 1). These categories are perceived in terms of dimension or degree instead of distinct categories. In other words, there is a spectrum of behaviors in each category that can be used in different settings or situations.

Table 1

Taxonomy of Leadership Behaviors

Category	Leadership Behaviors	Category	Leadership Behaviors
Task-oriented	Clarifying Planning Monitoring operations Problem Solving	Change-oriented	Advocating change Envisioning change Encouraging innovation Facilitation of collective learning
Relations-oriented	Supporting Developing Recognizing Empowering	External	Networking External monitoring Representing

From Yukl (2012)

Yukl also saw this taxonomy of behaviors as applicable to all types of leaders, regardless of hierarchy (Yukl, 2012). They developed a scale that included 13 behaviors across the three taxonomies to measure the presence and use of each behavior within an individual (Yukl, 2012). Additional researchers have validated and furthered this work. For example, Bish and Becker (2016) examined these behaviors in a specific nonprofit organizational context across multiple levels of leaders within an organization. They also identified two additional leadership skill areas that were relevant specifically to nonprofit organizations: personal knowledge and experience and nonprofit orientation. As these perspectives on leadership evolved in research, the view that leadership should be seen as independent of hierarchy has broadened (Schulze & Pinkow, 2020).

Other research validated Yukl's findings. Borgmann et al. (2016) analyzed over 280 studies that assessed Yukl's taxonomy, finding that the conceptual framework holds up across a broad review of the research literature. Another study using exploratory and confirmatory factor analysis to assess the use of his leadership behavior taxonomy on over 1000 managers across two industries lent additional credibility to the model (Özşahin, 2019).

Another characteristic of Yukl's taxonomy that distinguished it from the transformational–transactional dyad was the situational nature of leadership. In Yukl's view, all behaviors are relevant for leadership but are not equally relevant in all situations (Yukl et al., 2002). Timing can be a critical component for the use of specific skills (Yukl, 2012). This taxonomy also factors in the interdependence of behaviors that work together, either across or within categories (Yukl, 2012). This increased flexibility and situational nature of leadership paves the way for the role of shared leadership and reinforces the presence of leadership at multiple levels within an organization (Yukl, 2012).

Despite the seemingly comprehensive nature of Yukl's taxonomy of leadership behaviors, researchers continue to search for the best way to frame effective leadership models. A study by Behrendt et al. (2017) gives strength to Yukl's model, praising it as a *gold standard*; however, even with this commendation, Behrendt cites a relative weakness present in many models of leadership: there is little differentiation between actual behavior and the perception of behavior. As mentioned previously, this challenge with how leadership behavior is measured leads to a risk of confirmation bias in the observer (Behrendt et al., 2017). Behrendt's proposed

theory does not stray far from Yukl's model; the study collapses the original model into two

categories of task and relations-oriented behaviors, bolstered by the research of additional

theorists. A weakness of this model, however, is that it is still largely theoretical and has not been

validated through rigorous studies (Behrendt et al., 2017).

Complexity Leadership

The research of Yukl and others who viewed leadership behavior as contingent on

situational variables set the stage for complexity leadership (Uhl-Bien et al., 2007). Complexity

leadership supports an understanding of leader and follower behaviors within the modern

workplace (Uhl-Bien & Arena, 2018). Many organizations in the 21st century manage

knowledge instead of producing a product (Drucker, 2001; Uhl-Bien et al., 2007). Intellectual

property (or knowledge) and collaboration are key features of these systems. Complex adaptive

systems allow for leadership to be viewed as a process that occurs across all levels of an

organization (Uhl-Bien et al., 2007).

There are three major components of complexity leadership theory: entrepreneurial,

operational, and enabling leadership. Each one plays a unique role in the function of a complex

adaptive system (Uhl-Bien & Arena, 2018). Operational leadership provides structure to the

organization. It is probably the closest in image to more "traditional" leadership models of

providing rules and direction and draws parallels to the transactional leadership style. The role of

operational leadership is to provide constraints and demands on the system. In a sense, it helps to

create the boundaries for the system within which adaptive and enabling leadership play (Uhl-

Bien et al., 2007). Entrepreneurial leadership, in contrast, allows for changes in reaction to

events. It utilizes a situational approach to decision-making. Entrepreneurial leadership also embraces comfort with tension and encourages creativity in driving solutions (Uhl-Bien & Arena, 2018). Entrepreneurial leadership's focus on change and growth draws parallels to the transformational leadership style. Sitting between those two styles, enabling leadership stimulates balance between entrepreneurial and organizational leadership functions. It supports the flexibility within the system, allowing for bending and movement within the structure provided by operational frameworks but also focusing the creativity and tension that can surface from entrepreneurial leadership (Uhl-Bien et al., 2007). These types of leadership can be practiced by different individuals within a team structure or an individual may use elements of entrepreneurial, operational, and enabling leadership at different points of their work (Uhl-Bien & Arena, 2018; see Figure 3). It should be noted that earlier versions of Uhl-Bien's framework of complex adaptive systems used the terms *adaptive leadership* for *entrepreneurial leadership* and *administrative leadership* for *organizational leadership*. These were revised in 2018.

Figure 3

The Complexity Leadership Model

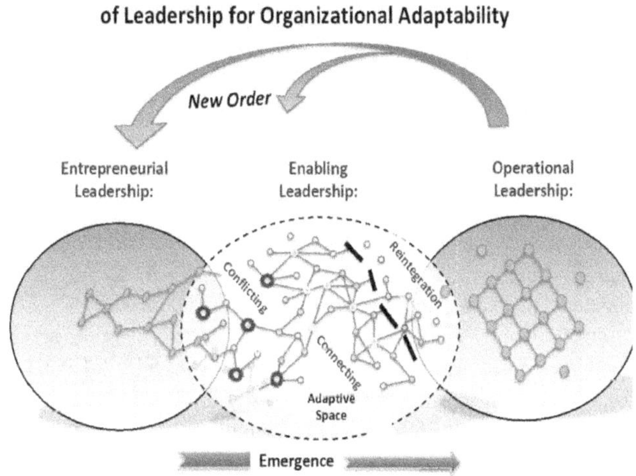

Reprinted from *The Leadership Quarterly*, Vol 29, Uhl-Bien & Arena, Leadership for

organizational adaptability: A theoretical synthesis and integrative framework, 89-104,

Copyright 2018, with permission from Elsevier.

Similar to the components of complexity leadership established by Uhl-Bien et al. (2007),

Zacher and Rosing (2015) identified *opening* and *closing* behaviors as a way to operationalize

the specific tasks that support nature of a leader's work. These opening and closing behaviors are

the key elements of ambidextrous leadership. For example, opening behaviors include those that

encourage brainstorming, long-term planning, and goal setting. In contrast, closing behaviors are

focused on task accomplishment or goal achievement (Zacher & Rosing, 2015).

Zacher and Rosing's quantitative survey research of Australian businesses revealed

through repeated surveys that the presence of both high opening and closing behaviors led to

high innovation in teams (Zacher & Rosing, 2015). In fact, they compared their rating scales

with the Multifactor Leadership Questionnaire (MLQ) as a standard against the use of a transformational leadership style. The study found that the opening and closing behaviors were more predictive for innovation than transformational leadership (Zacher & Rosing, 2015). A weakness of the study was a low response rate. While over 500 surveys were distributed to employee/manager teams for completion, the surveys only had a response rate of about 13%. This was due in part to the fact that both team leaders and their respective team members needed to return surveys for full study inclusion.

When they expanded this research 2 years later, the study design was adjusted to improve response rates. Using two separate quantitative designs: one conducted in Australia with 59 employees, and another conducted in Germany with 37 employees (Rosing & Zacher, 2017), the studies used daily and weekly surveys, resulting in 192 data points for study one and 156 data points for study two. Using multiple survey scales, including questionnaires that measured for innovation and affect, the research confirmed that individuals must engage in high and similar levels of opening and closing behaviors in order to achieve innovation (Rosing & Zacher, 2017).

The Core of Ambidextrous Organizations: Exploration and Exploitation

Adaptability is the key to modern organizational change. Managers and leaders play significant roles in organizational work (Uhl-Bien & Arena, 2018). Ambidexterity, at its core, is defined as the "capability to respond to changing environmental demands in a flexible way" (Sun et al., 2020, p. 556). In this way, leaders must simultaneously pursue efficiency and flexibility. There is always some degree of tension between the investment in an organization's future and refinement of their current work (Gibson & Birkinshaw, 2004). While ambidextrous leadership is defined through individual opening and closing behaviors, in a similar way organizational ambidexterity is defined through the use of exploration and exploitation (Havermans et al., 2015; Junni et al., 2013; Uhl-Bien & Arena, 2018). Much like opening behaviors, exploration behaviors are defined as involving others, stimulating discussion, expanding boundaries, and encouraging individual development. Exploitation behaviors include wariness, sticking to agreements, enforcing rules, and even stopping discussions. Havermans et al. (2015) identified these behaviors through 42 interviews with teams and project managers (see Table 2).

Junni et al. (2013) also identified a need for balance between exploration and exploitation to achieve true ambidexterity. Too much exploitation can lead to a "success trap": the organization adapts poorly to environmental changes. On the other hand, too much exploration leads to a "failure trap" where organizations drown under a pile of unfinished projects or ideas. Through their meta-analysis, Junni et al. (2013) found large differences in the way organizational ambidexterity has been measured in the literature, including variations on level of analysis and the industry in which it was measured. However, despite these differences, the overall results of the study indicated that organizational ambidexterity and performance are positively and significantly associated. An additional conclusion was that the relationship between organizational ambidexterity and performance was stronger when measured at more aggregate levels of an organization (downstream) as opposed to at the higher levels of the organization. Organizational ambidexterity allows teams to determine how they divide their time; when implemented correctly, organizational success follows (Koster & van Bree, 2018).

Table 2

Examples of Exploration and Exploitation Behaviors

	Leadership Behaviors
Exploration (Opening)	Involving others Stimulating discussion Expanding boundaries Encouraging individual development Availability
Exploitation (Closing)	Stopping discussion Wariness Sticking to agreements Enforcing rules

Adapted from Havermans et al. (2015)

Conceptualization of Ambidexterity: Multiple Perspectives

There are many conceptualizations of ambidexterity in research. This is due to variability in study execution and design (Popadić & Milohnić, 2016). The earliest research on ambidexterity began in the early 1990s; however, there was a peak of research from 2004-2014, with over 1800 citations and over 80 articles in 2014 alone that referred to organizational ambidexterity (Popadić & Milohnić, 2016). The majority of this research agreed that there is a need for balance between exploration and exploitation to achieve ambidexterity; however, there was disagreement on how to achieve it. There were often different measures used to quantify the use and mix of exploration and exploitation. Some studies looked at this in terms of addition while others looked at it in terms of difference or even a multiplicative effect (Junni et al., 2013; Popadić & Milohnić, 2016). For example, some organizations view ambidexterity as cycling through processes of exploration and exploitation based on environmental and temporal needs while others view ambidexterity as the simultaneous pursuit of both exploration and exploitation but in varying degrees, much like lines on a continuum (Popadić & Milohnić, 2016).

Ambidexterity within organizations is further delineated between structural, sequential, and contextual ambidexterity (Sun et al., 2020). These differences are often used and defined by project-based organizations. The researchers used multiple case analysis to study project-based organizations in China. They sampled seven extreme cases and identified three different types of organizational ambidexterity: contextual, structural, and sequential.

Contextual ambidexterity is defined as timely responses, flexibility, and having a faster rate of change; however, organizations that use contextual ambidexterity are also known for their unpredictability. Structural ambidexterity is frequently seen in strong matrix organizations with project teams. These groups use standard procedures to support changes and then offer tailored plans for each project. Authority is often designated to the project team and incentives are frequently used to improve team or individual performance. Sequential ambidexterity is typified by rapid but predictable changes. This also is used in matrix structures where teams often alternate with periods of dominance. There is a great deal of cross-team coordination. The lesson learned from these differing types of ambidexterity is that organizations must identify and understand their structural context and mission before selecting a specific ambidexterity approach (Sun et al., 2020). Case analyses by Popadić and Milohnić (2016) and Junni et al. (2013) support the view that the use of different kinds of organizational ambidexterity have equal value. While this creates some degree of theoretical ambiguity in the field, it also supports a case for equifinality: there are multiple routes to achieving a possible outcome and the decision-making process plays a role in the work (Cannaerts et al., 2020).

As mentioned previously, another hallmark of ambidexterity is the use of opening and closing behaviors by leadership. Multiple studies have identified characteristics of these behaviors through quantitative research, primarily utilizing regression analysis to compare opening and closing behaviors with ratings of transformational or transactional leadership, measures of team success, and other measures of innovation (Gerlach et al., 2020; Zacher & Rosing, 2015; Zacher et al., 2016). Opening behaviors are typified by creativity and the acquisition of new knowledge while closing behaviors involve goal setting, meeting of deadlines, and assessing for implementation needs. These behaviors are also often termed as exploration and exploitation behaviors in the literature. Opening or exploration behaviors tend to enhance innovation while closing or exploitation behaviors enhance production (March, 1991; Uhl-Bien & Arena, 2018).

March (1991) was one of the first to posit the concept of exploration and exploitation behaviors in organizational learning. March emphasized a collective role in the ambidexterity process, acknowledging that there is always competition for ideas. March proposed a mathematical model to quantify the unique roles of exploration and exploitation in organizational development; however, these ideas were based on a closed system and were more theoretical than practical. One strong implication from March's research, however, was that higher rates of learning resulted in an achievement of equilibrium in ambidexterity earlier. This implies that diverse (and possibly shared) leadership leads to greater depth and breadth of exploration and exploitation in practice within an organization.

Finding a balance in using these opening and closing behaviors can be challenging. Zimmerman et al. (2018) concluded that tension is often a natural part of the ambidexterity process. While senior managers can set the tone for managing these tensions, it is often frontline managers who must balance top-down and bottom-up decision making. This conclusion was echoed by Bish and Becker (2016) in their examination of nonprofit managers in varying roles across an organization.

Zacher and Rosing (2015) examined these behaviors in 33 leaders and 90 of their employees in team situations and found that opening and closing behaviors were a better predictor for innovation than transformational leadership. There were some weaknesses in the study, including a small sample and a newer scale used to measure opening/closing behaviors, which may have impacted the construct validity. The researchers were concerned that team ratings might be biased, and that team functioning was not considered. However, further study extended this research and looked at ambidexterity at the interindividual (employee) level (Zacher et al., 2016). Improvements in this study included a large sample (388 employees) and improved controls for transformational and transactional leadership as well as other performance variables. This expanded study again found a predictive relationship between opening and closing behaviors on innovation that went above and beyond transformational or transactional leadership styles in isolation. A major conclusion of the study was that there is an overlapping but inconsistent relationship between exploration/exploitation behaviors and the transformational/transactional leadership styles (Zacher et al., 2016). While many elements of the transformational leadership style align with exploration behaviors and elements of the transactional leadership style often align with exploitation behaviors, ambidextrous leadership is not seen in a binary or static context with respect to *use of style*. Instead, it is the interplay and use of exploration and exploitation at key moments within a team's work that sparks effectiveness and innovation. For this reason, it is incumbent on leaders to develop an awareness of how they use exploration and exploitation within their teams in order to enhance employee performance (Zacher et al., 2016). This understanding guides leaders as they allocate and utilize staff support over time within the organization for the purposes of innovation or production.

Rosing and Zacher (2017) expanded this work again to conduct a 2-part study to look at the use of these behaviors for innovation in individuals. A major conclusion of the study is that individuals must engage in both high and similar levels of exploration and exploitations behaviors in order to achieve innovation (Rosing & Zacher, 2017). The study also differentiates innovation from creativity in that innovation involves not just the creation of but the *implementation of* ideas. A final important conclusion is that the individual, cross-organizational level nature of the study demonstrated the importance of ambidexterity beyond the leader level and to all areas of an organization. This study was strengthened by larger sample sizes, robust controls for research reliability, and high reliability of results through repetition.

More recently, Gerlach et al. (2020) achieved similar results while looking at the behaviors of 54 German employees in various for-profit industries over the course of 6 weeks. The researchers used multi-level random intercept regression analysis, which allowed them to look at both between-person and within-person measures for opening and closing behaviors and innovation. A major conclusion of the study reaffirmed the previous study by Rosing and Zacher (2017) that high opening and closing behaviors are associated with innovation.

While there seem to be limited quantitative tools for specifically measuring leader support on innovation, Vincent-Höper and Stein (2019) conducted an extensive study in developing a tool known as the Leader Support for Innovation Questionnaire (LSIQ). The tool was developed using two samples from Germany and South Africa involving a total of 1,062 employees, 54% of whom were female. The tool was validated in both German and English and met requirements for factorial validity, incremental validity, and construct validity, including a Cronbach's alpha of > .85 for all measures. Further, results were explained beyond and differentiated from transformational leadership or leadership membership exchange styles

(Vincent-Höper & Stein, 2019).

The LSIQ is a 12-item survey that measures three factors of leader support on a 5-point

Likert scale: idea generation, idea promotion, and idea implementation. Leaders may engage in

complementary behaviors to promote innovation. In short, it is often achieved through a

nonlinear process. While it is still a relatively novel tool, the role of the LSIQ may be to give

leaders feedback about their potential to support others within team environments (Vincent-

Höper & Stein, 2019).

Connecting Ambidexterity and Complexity from a Qualitative Perspective

There is a connection between complexity leadership and other shared leadership models

(Havermans et al., 2015; Routhieaux, 2015; Uhl-Bien et al., 2007). Leaders fulfill many roles

within organizations, including the development, evaluation, and facilitation of their members.

For this reason, qualitative research often supports identification of key behaviors and strategies

that leaders use in different organizational environments (Bouwmans et al., 2019; Gilstrap et al.,

2016; Severgnini et al., 2019; Uhl-Bien & Arena, 2018).

Bouwmans et al. (2019) investigated how team leaders in vocational schools in the

Netherlands use processes with teaching teams. Their qualitative research with 11 teachers in

individual and group interviews revealed that a variety or combination of styles are used by team

leaders. The differences in styles were very context dependent or situational, determined largely

by the skills and needs of the team as well as the leader's own style (Bouwmans et al., 2019).

Leaders often differed in their use of human resource management processes and the

perception of control and fit with the team also played a role in the leader's individual perception

of both control and commitment (Bouwmans et al., 2019). Although Mulenga et al. (2018) used a transformational leadership style conceptual framework, they similarly found that leaders use multiple practices in working with teams, including networking, communication, and performance appraisals. Mulenga et al. (2018) also found that leaders impact the individuals they manage by providing confidence, motivation, resources, and guidance. A grounding conclusion in their research was that a combination of styles was used but the way that a leader implements these different skills and tactics can have an impact on service delivery (Mulenga et al., 2018).

A meta-synthesis case study by Severgnini et al. (2019) also reinforced the underlying concept that a combination of exploration and exploitation behaviors by leaders are used in regular practice. The study's conclusion was that analysis of risk may be a key component of decision making. Havermans et al. (2015) also found that the balance between exploration and exploitation constantly shifts. Their qualitative study examined these specific behaviors in the context of 42 teams and their project managers (see Table 2). Their findings revealed not only the different aspects of exploration and exploitation behaviors but that the use of these behaviors in project-based organizations was critical to finding a balance between efficiency and innovation.

Role of Enabling Leadership

Within the ambidexterity model, enabling leaders must work to create spaces for tension to occur (Schulze & Pinkow, 2020; Uhl-Bien, 2021; Uhl-Bien & Arena, 2018). These tensions can be structural, decisional, or hierarchical (Peng, 2019). Tensions often emerge as a system is pushed out of equilibrium; enabling leadership encourages these competing ideas to collide through facilitation, reorganization, and networking to share ideas and resources (Uhl-Bien, 2021). Schulze and Pinkow (2020) investigated the use of enabling leadership through qualitative interviews with six people working in management consulting firms. Their analysis revealed that it is the responsibility of leaders to create space for this work.

There are three primary areas of behavior where enabling leaders consistently work (Schulze & Pinkow, 2020). First, they use an innovation approach to continually support and scale new ideas. This keeps the operationalizing of administrative leadership in check. Next, they create adaptive spaces by fostering diversity and providing flexibility for how the work is done. Finally, they connect individuals and concepts within the work setting to external environments, integrating these connections into the organization's current needs. They also foster connections by encouraging broad networks and group cohesion.

Another example of the role that enabling leadership can play in sustainable development can be found in fair-trade systems (Simeoni et al., 2020). These economic systems often utilize secondary organizations that act as a bridge between the fair-trade suppliers and the larger economic system. Using a qualitative approach, Simeoni et al. (2020) found that these intermediary organizations play a crucial role in providing ambidexterity tools that are necessary for the success and sustainability of the fair-trade system. Specifically, they can provide a framework for flexibility and structure between the two groups and foster collaboration between groups with similar aims but sometimes differing approaches to economic development and need. Although the Italian study looked at a very specific economic context, elements of the model can be applicable to other hybrid business models and nonprofit collaborations (Simeoni et al., 2020).

Koster and van Bree (2018) also found that managers use specific mechanisms to create conditions that promote exploration and exploitation through collaboration. They researched this in the context of a Dutch hospital through qualitative interviews with 13 individuals across multiple levels of the organization. Koster and van Bree found similar themes around collaboration, trust, and flexibility. Additionally, they identified that ambidexterity is a process that must be subjected to constant review. The tension and obstacles differ as a matter of degree and the presence of management is very important. Although the scope of the study was limited in looking only at a small Dutch hospital, the themes resonated with other qualitative research, particularly that of Schulze and Pinkow (2020) and Peng (2019). While all of these studies were limited in their scope on a small population, each contributes to our understanding that the role enabling leadership plays in working with tension, fostering diversity, creating flexibility, and approaching obstacles in a new way through collaboration resonates and sets the stage for situational factors that impact leadership style. Enabling leadership drives the continual interplay between leaders (or within a leader utilizing multiple styles) to balance the needs for innovation and production within the organization (Bolden et al., 2020; Uhl-Bien & Arena, 2018).

Situational Factors Impacting Ambidextrous Leadership

There are specific situational factors that have been identified in impacting the use of ambidextrous leadership within organizations. Severgnini et al. (2019) concluded that analyzing risk may be a key part of decision making by leadership in organizations. The study was a meta-synthesis that examined eight research studies (from an initial pool of 51). Each study examined how risk exerted a moderating effect on the use of exploration and exploitation behaviors within organizations. Key takeaways from the case synthesis were that exploration was used more often in low risk situations and exploitation was used more often in high risk situations (Severgnini et al., 2019). An analysis of risk may be a key component in leader decision making. It is also important to note that risk and uncertainty may not be equal. These findings connect with research previously brought forward by Uhl-Bien et al. (2007) and Havermans et al. (2015) that the role of exploration and exploitation is constantly shifting within an organization and that an optimum balance depends heavily on environmental influences.

Time pressure also can play a role in leadership style. Dóci et al. (2020) looked at a total of over 500 daily questionnaires completed by 42 Belgian leaders who worked in a variety of private sector leadership roles. Their research found that a variety or combination of styles were used by team leaders and the style chosen was very context dependent. Determining factors included the skills and needs of the team as well as the leader's own style. Leaders often differed in their use of human resource management processes over time. The perception of control and fit with the team played a role in perceptions of both control and commitment. This study added to the body of literature by examining within person changes rather than between person differences (Dóci et al., 2020). Further, the study reinforced findings by Valero and colleagues (2015) that a significant relationship exists between the use of a transformational leadership style and organizational resiliency. In fact, personnel capacity played a greater role in resiliency during times of crisis than financial capacity. Valero et al. (2015) concluded from this research that *more personnel* does not always equal the *best personnel*. Both studies conclude that specific training and investment in existing leaders can enhance organizational stability during times of crisis or challenge.

Gilstrap et al. (2016) specifically examined the role that crisis plays in leadership capacity in the nonprofit sector. Using a grounded theory approach, 43 nonprofit leaders whose organizations had been impacted by a major environmental crisis (e.g., hurricane, oil spill, etc.) were interviewed. Characteristics that were identified as key to effective management included: being a team player, exhibiting transparency and composure, strategic thinking, quick responses, and exhibiting preparedness. Gilstrap et al. (2016) also identified a framework that incorporated instrumental knowledge, normalcy, and dynamic learning in supporting organizational goals during times of crisis.

Similarly, Park and Mosley (2017) looked at key leader behaviors in youth-serving nonprofit organizations during times of economic uncertainty. Several themes emerged from the interviews. Strong leaders demonstrated diversification, advocacy, accountability, and a strong management background. While these themes drew some similarities to that of other research (Gilstrap et al., 2016; Witmer & Mellinger, 2016), the study was unclear in its rigor of analysis or method and the scope of the study was a limited sample of organizations from one geographic region of the United States (Chicago, IL).

Significant organizational change can also play a role in leadership behaviors. Yahaya (2020) examined mid-level manager behaviors and reactions to organizational change in nonprofit home care organizations. This study was unique in that other research often engages high-level leaders or looks at leadership across multiple levels of an organization. Through in-depth interviews, Yahaya identified four main themes that were experienced by these mid-level managers during organizational change: stress and fear, job dissatisfaction, employee exclusion, and task-oriented leader behavior. Most of these themes revealed that organizational change is perceived negatively at the mid-manager level and communication challenges are a big part of this perception. A weakness of this study (or an opportunity for future research) is that the study was heavily focused on the challenges of organizational change; however, there was little insight into solutions or opportunities where leaders could work to ameliorate these negative perceptions.

Nonprofit Sector Organizational Needs

The nonprofit sector accounts for 10% of the U.S. workforce and is the third largest employer (NCCS, 2020). As nonprofit organizations are increasingly called to develop a business focus, questions arise as to whether the skill set of nonprofit leaders may be different from those in the for-profit workforce (Aboramadan & Kundi, 2020; Bish & Becker, 2016). As a business sector, nonprofit organizations face unique challenges with organizational management, human services management, and leadership considerations. Because of its primary focus on service to the greater community, a nonprofit's performance is frequently assessed on mission outcomes more than on financial returns (Collins, 2005).

One key challenge facing organizations in the nonprofit sector is the ability to build capacity (Zhang et al., 2017). Organizational capacity is the key to growth and "an organization's ability to solve problems and achieve goals" (Zhang et al., 2017, p. 429). Unlike for-profit businesses, which frequently have opportunities to expand and grow through financing and venture capital, nonprofit organizations are often stretched to their limit for resources (Gregory & Howard, 2009). Relying on restricted sources of funding such as grants or designated donations, there is a priority placed on program deliverables tied specifically to grant outcomes with often little flexibility given to administrators for the use of such collateral. In fact, grants rarely support capacity building or administrative support necessary for growth and innovation (Zhang et al., 2017).

It is also important to note that funding sources and needs can differ even within the nonprofit sector (Collins, 2005; Wyman, 2018). This can be visualized as four quadrants where organizations are viewed on a continuum of low/high reliance on public support and low/high reliance on business revenue (see Figure 4). For example, public schools, police, and other government funded entities have low reliance on both public support and business revenue (Quadrant I) while hospitals and state universities often rely heavily on business revenue but less on public support (Quadrant IV). Organizations such as churches and human service causes (such as the Special Olympics) rely heavily on public supports and grants but minimally on business revenue (Quadrant II) and private universities, arts organizations, and groups such as the Girl Scouts rely on high levels of both public support and business revenue (Quadrant III). Because of these differences, the strategy for ongoing funding and capacity building may vary greatly across the nonprofit sector (Wyman, 2018).

Figure 4

The Economic Engines of the Nonprofit Sector

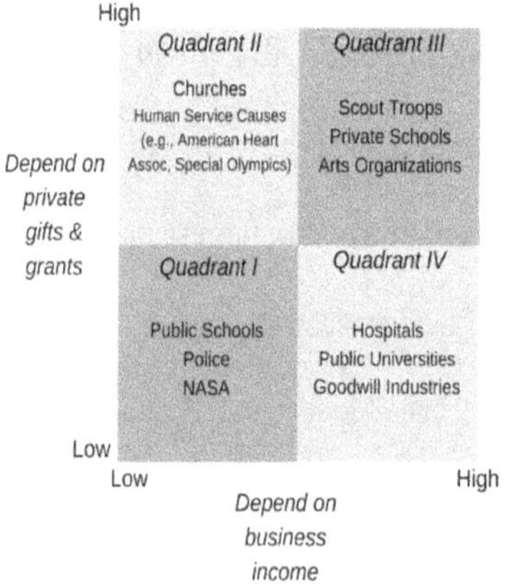

Adapted from Collins (2005)

What is true across the board is that nonprofit organizations are historically asked to do more with less (Peng, 2019). They frequently operate in a starvation cycle with an understood need to perpetually conserve any available resources (Gregory & Howard, 2009). Operating in a scarcity mindset is more the rule than the exception for organizations. A 2018 report on the fiscal health of the nonprofit sector revealed that 50% of organizations have less than 1 month of cash reserves; 30% had lost money over the previous 3 years; and 7-8% of organizations are technically insolvent (Wyman, 2018).

Local and global economic factors frequently only serve to exacerbate these challenges. The most recent COVID-19 pandemic is a prime example. While research is still ongoing, a 2021 survey of 163 nonprofit organizations by the Center for Effective Philanthropy found that most leaders reported significant negative impacts on funding, programming, and staffing due to the Covid-19 pandemic (Martin et al., 2021). Eighty-eight percent (88%) of organizations had altered their program offerings in the previous year, 58% had to reduce programs or services, 38% had to dip into their financial reserves, and 31% laid off or furloughed employees.

As stewards of public and private funding, nonprofit organizations are subject to accountability standards often not shared with their for-profit counterparts (Routhieaux, 2015; Wyman, 2018). These standards can be challenging to measure because they deliver a service rather than a "product"; their intention is rarely to produce goods at a profit (Becker, 2018). As mentioned previously, the restrictive nature of funding through grants can often limit organizational innovation and sustainability (Wyman, 2018). Due to all these factors, nonprofits are increasingly asked to deliver programs and services in a socially innovative way (Shier & Handy, 2020).

Nonprofit Sector Leadership Needs

While it is acknowledged that leadership and organizational capacity needs for nonprofits are different, these contexts are not studied with the same rigor in organizational leadership research as their for-profit counterparts (Aboramadan & Kundi, 2020; Brimhall, 2021).

Many factors impact leadership effectiveness within a nonprofit organization. Bish and Becker (2016) conducted a qualitative case study of 21 managers across three (3) hierarchical levels in a large Australian nonprofit. Utilizing Yukl's taxonomy of leadership behaviors (Yukl, 2012) their research revealed that many factors impact leadership effectiveness within a nonprofit organization. Expectations of leaders differed across levels for certain tasks. In fact, the position of a leader within the hierarchy may be the best indicator of the types of skills that are most helpful to support the organization. As an addition to the body of research, Bish and Becker identified two additional leadership skill areas that were relevant to nonprofit organizations: personal knowledge and experience and nonprofit orientation. (Bish & Becker, 2016).

The role of different leadership styles can vary even within different nonprofit sector organizations. Fazzi and Zamaro (2016) explored the relationship between leadership styles in public service organizations compared to nonprofits focused on research (such as universities). While both transformational and transactional leadership styles were utilized by leaders in both types of organizations, transformational leadership exerted more control over leaders in public service organizations than transactional leadership. In the research focused organizations, transactional leadership styles exerted negative control on motivation in employees. This may be because researchers often value autonomy and flexibility in their work, so a transactional style may come across as too managerial or directive (Fazzi & Zamaro, 2016). A guiding conclusion of the research was that leaders must be able to read organizational contexts and alter their leadership style based on situational variables, the needs of the organization, and the needs of the people whom they lead.

Cross-sector partnerships, including collaborations between organizations, are a large part of nonprofit work (Shier & Handy, 2016, 2020). Collaboration can provide efficiency, sustainability, and greater community participation. However, these inherent needs for collaboration can often lead to complexity and time lag in decision making or action (Collins, 2005). These challenges often present logistical and operational barriers for nonprofit organizations and it is incumbent on organizational leaders to be mindful of this when engaging in strategic planning.

Shier and Handy's qualitative research identified key factors for leaders who successfully engage in these types of partnerships. These included highly structured engagement with stakeholders, clear alignment of partners and aims, and a focus on interpersonal dynamics (Shier & Handy, 2016). An extension of this study additionally revealed two key themes as integral to successful nonprofit partnerships: an orientation to partnership (strong engagement) and a focus on internal stakeholder engagement (Shier & Handy, 2020). This was demonstrated through more horizontal management structures, opportunities for teams to dream and plan, and a structure for shared decision making. These findings reinforced and extended similar research conducted by Bish and Becker (2016) on a single nonprofit organization in that the study examined specific behaviors that led to successful nonprofit collaborations. The Shier and Handy study also reflected research on enabling leadership (Koster & van Bree, 2018; Peng, 2019; Schulze & Pinkow, 2020); however, it used a leadership framework based in transformational and transactional dyad styles rather than one based in the ambidexterity model (Uhl-Bien et al., 2007). It should also be noted that all of the organizations sampled by Shier and Handy had partnerships with government organizations and public agencies. They were also older and well-established (25 years+ of history), so it is unclear whether these findings are transferable to younger organizations or those in other human services sectors.

Nonprofit leaders must balance separation and connection when challenged to lead diverse organizations (Regan, 2016). Further, leaders who cross sectors successfully (from nonprofit to public and vice versa) also demonstrate specific skill capabilities (Austin et al., 2012). They are frequently seen as client advocates, organizational change agents, and team leaders who are particularly skilled at problem solving. This research also identified that leaders who crossed sectors in their careers had an expanded perspective compared to counterparts working in more homogeneous organizational environments (Austin et al., 2012).

In addition to cross-organization collaboration, a shared leadership model is often seen within nonprofit organizations, most frequently in the relationship between the executive director and the board chair (Hodge & Piccolo, 2011; Routhieaux, 2015;). Nonprofit organizations that use a shared leadership model are often better positioned for sustainability (Routhieaux, 2015). Similarly, in a survey of 112 nonprofit organizations, Hodge and Piccolo (2011) found that there is a relationship between board activity and nonprofit financial success. While not specifically examining a nonprofit context, this was reinforced by Junni et al. (2013), which found that organizational ambidexterity and performance were stronger at levels where collaboration was more likely to occur.

Ambidexterity in the Nonprofit Sector

The role of ambidexterity on organizational performance is clear. The question that remains is not whether ambidexterity exists in organizational contexts but, rather, *when* and *how* ambidexterity is utilized by leaders (Junni et al., 2013). Junni et al. (2013) further warns that applying organizational ambidexterity study results from one industry to another may not be valid. Nonprofit organizations must keep both accountability and work towards social value top of mind in their strategy and implementation plans, and these needs align well with an ambidextrous approach (Peng, 2019). However, the complexity of ambidextrous leadership also begs a question of cost benefit since high levels of exploration and exploitation in a nonprofit environment are often necessary for success (Junni et al., 2013). Recent research has explored the concept of ambidexterity in nonprofit contexts, either explicitly or implicitly, using a variety of contexts and research aims. The following sections will introduce research on ambidexterity based on: fostering resilience, work engagement and innovation, connection to the lifecycle of the organization, cross-sector partnerships, and civic governance and public organizations.

Fostering Resilience

Resilience is a key component of nonprofit sustainability (Dóci et al., 2020; Gilstrap et al., 2016; Routhieaux, 2015; Valero et al., 2015; Witmer & Mellinger, 2016). It is demonstrated in the organization's ability to adapt to circumstances. Witmer and Mellinger (2016) specifically addressed resilience through a qualitative study of two behavioral healthcare organizations. Interviewing individuals at multiple levels of the organization, the researchers found that leaders need key components for sustainability:

- Commitment to the organization and mission

- Improvisation in using existing resources

- Reciprocal relationships within the community

- A perspective of hope and optimism

- A servant or transformational leadership style

- Fiscal transparency

While the study only examined one particular industry, it identified components that could be explored further, particularly through a context of ambidextrous leadership.

Work Engagement and Innovation

Work engagement has also been identified as a predictor for affective commitment in a nonprofit context (Aboramadan & Kundi, 2020). This quantitative study used the transformational–transactional leadership dyad for their theoretical framework instead of an ambidexterity framework. While transformational leadership was identified as the most effective leadership style for generating follower commitment, the research revealed that transactional leadership should not be discounted. This reinforced previous research that leadership styles should not be examined in isolation (Judge & Piccolo, 2004). Brimhall (2021) conducted a similar study that virtually replicated Aboramadan and Kundi's (2020) conclusions with a different sample. While the first study was conducted in Italy with 555 nonprofit employees, Brimhall's sample included 300 employees from a nonprofit hospital in the United States. Brimhall also found that more research is needed to determine how nonprofit leaders can leverage human capital for innovation. A unifying conclusion from both studies is that transformational leadership creates a climate for inclusion, which increases overall affective commitment and innovation on behalf of employees (Aboramadan & Kundi, 2020; Brimhall, 2021). An extension of this research could examine work engagement and innovation using an ambidextrous leadership conceptual framework in a similar nonprofit context.

Connection to the Lifecycle of an Organization

A constant principle of ambidextrous leadership is the situational role that context plays in moderating a leader's style or strategy; however, very little of this research has been conducted in nonprofit contexts (Bouwmans et al., 2019; Gerlach et al., 2020; Uhl-Bien et al., 2007; Uhl-Bien & Arena, 2018). Rojas (2018) used a grounded theory approach to look at the factors that impact leadership decisions in faith-based organizations (Catholic parishes) with respect to the life cycle of each parish. Rojas's research revealed a pastoral life cycle model that can inform church leaders as to what types of leadership styles are best suited to these life cycle stages. For example, a church welcoming a new priest (transitioning in) may require a more transactional style of leadership than a church in a more mature "nurturing" stage where a priest is serving a growing and thriving congregation. In this setting a more transformational style tied in to relational interactions would better align with congregational needs (Rojas, 2018). This research, tying specific leadership strategies to the life cycle of the organization, is aligned closely with other work done by Kenny-Stevens (2008). While an ambidextrous leadership model does not always specifically tie into the life cycle of an organization, the contextual nature of ambidexterity and regular assessment of needs for exploration and exploitation both align with a life cycle framework (Uhl-Bien & Arena, 2018).

Cross-Sector Partnerships

Within the nonprofit sector, there are characteristics of leadership that support social innovation (Shier & Handy, 2016, 2020). As mentioned earlier, these studies examined the role of nonprofit leadership through the context of collaboration, the first study (2016) looked at 31 Canadian organizations and the later study (2020) had a sample of 31 leaders representing organizations in Pennsylvania (USA) via qualitative interviews. Both studies identified that partnership orientation (external engagement) and internal stakeholder engagement are keys to innovation in the social (nonprofit) sector. This can be fostered in leaders by creating more horizontal team management structures, building in opportunities for leaders to dream and plan, and being open to ideas utilizing models of shared decision making (Shier & Handy, 2020).

While the focus of these studies is shared leadership, the researchers did not use a conceptual framework that specifically identified ambidexterity. Instead, the focus was more on environmental factors that mediate or moderate a model that utilizes transformational and transactional leadership styles. In this way, it was similar to the research done by Aboramadan and Kundi (2020) and Brimhall (2021).

Role in Civic Governance and Public Organizations

Given the collaborative nature of civic organizations with public work, ambidexterity plays a central role in many nonprofits that work to influence policy and exact change within communities. Current systems thinking in public administration involves a shift away from hierarchical systems to more flat or integrated systems (Bolden et al., 2020). The challenge often lies in identifying the type of problem immediately and framing it to develop a plan grounded in systems thinking. Simple problems require management, messy problems with no obvious solution require leadership and critical problems (requiring rapid action) may need a more autocratic style. The facilitation practices identified in Bolden et al.'s study were similar to the enabling leadership practices identified by Uhl-Bien and Arena (2018).

Mathews (2020) studied the collaborative nature of leadership through 17 executive director–board chair dyads in a metropolitan area. While the study only examined one civic system, the themes that emerged included the importance of a shared leadership model, facilitating participation from the community, and finding a balance between managing conflict and empowering others. This management of tension, while not specifically named as such in Mathews' study, echoed the Uhl-Bien et al. (2007) conceptualization of the role of enabling leadership that is inherent in ambidexterity models.

Peng (2019) explored these concepts of ambidexterity in public organizations through a case study of a French organization. Peng's observations and interviews, although limited in scope, also honed in on the tensions inherent in collaborative work. A constant balance in changes between timing and resources, decision making, and innovation or adaptation must be considered by leaders over time. It is the role of leaders to balance and manage those tensions. Peng concluded that "an ambidextrous vision favors the search for balanced solutions" (Peng, 2019, p. 258).

Research Approach

The role that ambidextrous leadership plays in the success of an organization has been examined in both quantitative and qualitative research contexts. Recent research utilized both case study (Peng, 2019) and grounded theory (Gilstrap et al., 2016; Rojas, 2018; Shier & Handy, 2020) approaches to better understand the role of leadership behaviors within nonprofit organizations.

As a research methodology, grounded theory emerged from a need to pursue knowledge using a pragmatic approach (Charmaz, 2014). This knowledge and understanding emerges from the interaction between the researcher, the subjects under study, and the overarching context of history and research practice (Hunter et al., 2011).

The grounded theory research approach examines relationships between concepts and supports a conceptual framework grounded in a process (Creswell & Poth, 2018; Maxwell, 2013). Grounded theory also acknowledges that multiple factors may influence a final outcome to a problem and supports that exploration in a conceptual way. The search for practical solutions to world problems, particularly in human services work such as education, healthcare, and other fields dominated by nonprofit organizations, can frequently be facilitated by the use of grounded theory (Hunter et al., 2011).

Summary

Models of leadership effectiveness have evolved over time as the understanding of leadership has changed (Burke, 2018; Mintzberg, 2009; Sashkin & Burke, 1990). As workplaces become increasingly collaborative, there is recognition that leadership occurs at all levels of an organization (Uhl-Bien et al., 2007).

While historically the transformational and transactional leadership styles were seen as a gold standard leadership model, newer thinking by Yukl and others provided an understanding of leadership based on specific behaviors along a continuum, based on situational variables (Yukl, 2012). This idea opened the doors for complexity leadership. In complex systems, leaders may use a variety of styles in different contexts to perform functions of administration, adaptation, and to enable the balance between the two (Uhl-Bien et al., 2007).

Ambidexterity is defined as the simultaneous use of exploration and exploitation to pursue a balance of innovation and production (Sun et al., 2020). This balance can occur through shared leadership or through the ambidextrous nature of leaders adapting to environmental variables (Havermans et al., 2015; Uhl-Bien et al., 2007).

While ambidexterity has been studied in many different contexts, the nonprofit sector has explored this subject in a limited way (Aboramadan & Kundi, 2020; Brimhall, 2021). Nonprofit organizations use shared leadership models and are required to frequently adapt to new environments due to fiscal and organizational capacity challenges (Gilstrap et al., 2016; Witmer & Mellinger, 2016). Some studies have identified characteristics of ambidextrous leadership in nonprofit organizations (Koster & van Bree, 2018; Peng, 2019; Shier & Handy, 2020). However, these characteristics have often been measured through narrow contexts such as faith-based institutions (Rojas, 2018), single municipalities or organizations (Mathews, 2020; Peng, 2019), or stable organizations with long histories (Shier & Handy, 2020).

More research is needed to understand the role ambidextrous leadership plays in nonprofit organizations of varying sizes or developmental needs. Specifically, there is a need to understand which exploration and exploitation (opening and closing) behaviors are most supportive to a nonprofit organization's need for innovation or production. Additionally, it is important to understand how leaders use the principles of ambidextrous leadership to collaborate and utilize a shared leadership model, either within their own organization or in partnership with other community groups.

Chapter 3: Research Design and Method

Chapter Overview

The purpose of this qualitative study was to understand the skills and knowledge that nonprofit leaders utilize to manage the varied needs of their respective organizations. Ambidextrous leadership uses situational responses to facilitate opportunities within the organization for innovation or production (Sun et al., 2020). As nonprofit leaders are called to balance current capacity with the need to drive their mission, the use of ambidextrous leadership is vital to success (Zhang et al., 2017). I explored this topic using a grounded theory approach that utilized individual, semistructured interviews with nonprofit leaders. Interview questions explored the perceptions leaders have of using an ambidextrous style, the role of joint space in organizational strategy, and specific tactics that support a leader's balance between seeking innovation and production. Transcripts of the recorded interviews were analyzed for themes. This chapter covers the rationale and design for the research study, including a review of the research questions. Specific methodology, instrumentation, and data processing procedures will be described. Ethical considerations, considerations for validity, assumptions, and limitations inherent to the study are also included.

Research Questions

The primary research question under investigation for this study was: how do nonprofit leaders use ambidextrous leadership practices to support their organization's unique needs for innovation and production?

The following subquestions were also addressed:

1. How do nonprofit leaders use elements of ambidextrous leadership to collaborate with other organizations or utilize a shared leadership model?

2. What elements of ambidextrous leadership are most supportive to a nonprofit organization's need for innovation?

3. What elements of ambidextrous leadership are most supportive to a nonprofit organization's need for production?

Research Design

The selection of a research approach is driven by three primary factors: the researcher's worldview (or epistemology) related to knowledge and understanding, the overall research design, and the method chosen for the pursuit of specific research questions (Creswell, 2018).

Epistemology and Worldview

Philosophical perspectives play an important role in research. The way a researcher understands their world defines their approach to solving problems (Bechara & Van de Ven, 2007). Some approaches to knowledge are subjective: knowledge is impermanent and constructed based on a current state or place in the world. Knowledge can change based on the perspective of the person taking in information. Other approaches rely on empirical objectivity. Knowledge can only be gained based on what is found through empirical evidence and rigorous experimentation. Most people fall somewhere on this objective-subjective continuum with respect to their philosophy of science.

My own epistemology stems from a combination of critical realism and pragmatism. This view believes that knowledge is objectively assessed, but it is also influenced by personal knowledge and preferences (Jones, 2008). The pragmatic view combines the role of both subjective and objectives perspectives (Bechara & Van de Ven, 2007). Evidence is considered within the context of changing realities and personal views. The critical realist view also acknowledges the impact of the role of an observer within any research situation, exerting even small influences over the knowledge that is gained simply based on their presence (Jones, 2008).

When approaching a research question, the pragmatist often aims for solutions that are rooted in practical outcomes (Bechara & Van de Ven, 2007). They also often rely on an a priori framework based on previous research. For these reasons, a qualitative grounded theory approach aligned well with both my personal epistemology and the research questions under investigation.

Qualitative Approach

Pragmatic approaches can lean in a positivist direction, searching for empirical truth. This would sometimes point the research in a quantitative direction (Creswell, 2018). However, not all research questions can be answered in a quantitative way. The quantitative approach examines the relationship between variables while a qualitative approach is helpful when examining a process (Maxwell, 2013). Instead of thinking in terms of causal conditions, a qualitative approach acknowledges that many factors may influence an effect (Shadish et al., 2002). The qualitative approach applies sensitivity to tune in to connections between prior knowledge and newly discovered information (Corbin & Strauss, 2015).

The Grounded Theory Approach

Qualitative methods are relatively new to social science research (Kenny & Fourie, 2014). When Glaser and Strauss developed the grounded theory methodology in the 1960s, it was partly because they approached research with a pragmatic (and sometimes even positivist) epistemology but realized that quantitative methods did not fully serve their purposes in accomplishing their research aims (Corbin & Strauss, 2015).

In grounded theory, the focus is on a process (Creswell & Poth, 2018; Hunter et al., 2011; Maxwell, 2013). Data or information is pulled from the field (typically via interviews) and the theory is generated by discovered themes (Creswell & Poth, 2018). In this approach, context becomes a key component or understanding (Maxwell, 2013). The iterative coding process and reflexive generation of themes allows for the identification of influences in a flexible way.

Another way this research approach aligns with pragmatism is that it is grounded in acts of daily life (Hunter et al., 2011). Often the grounded theorist seeks practical solutions to world problems. The approach is frequently used in fields such as education, healthcare, and human services work. Finally, the grounded theory approach acknowledges the role that the researcher plays in the work (Hunter et al., 2011). Memoing, journaling, and a constant reflection between data previously collected and information most recently discovered are all part of the grounded theory analysis process.

Grounded Theory Over Time

As the field of grounded theory developed, it evolved beyond Glaser & Strauss's initial approach in key ways. The original model of grounded theory advocated for avoiding the research literature and exploring the research questions without a need to understand what had come before (Kenny & Fourie, 2014). However, both Straussian and constructed grounded theory approaches acknowledge the need for an understanding of history. Corbin explained this as the difference between an *open mind* and an *empty mind* (Hunter et al., 2011).

This role of context is important particularly to these newer approaches, as it places the theory in context of factors such as time and culture (Hunter et al., 2011). The theory is constructed through interaction between history, people, and research practice (Charmaz, 2014; Kenny & Fourie, 2014). In constructed grounded theory, Charmaz (2014) acknowledged the subjectivity that works in congress with a pragmatic worldview to assess a problem in context. It pulls from the roots of classic grounded theory approaches with emphasis on "action and meaning inherent in the pragmatist tradition" (Charmaz, 2014, p. 13). However, constructed grounded theory also goes a step beyond Straussian approaches, espousing that truth is only true when it is built together (by the researcher and their subjects). My own approach to the research, grounded in both critical realism and pragmatism, reflects a Straussian model of grounded theory.

Population and Sample

The population under investigation for this study were individuals who work in leadership roles in nonprofit organizations. Recruitment focused heavily on nonprofit leaders in the metropolitan area of Richmond, Virginia; however, this eligibility criteria was not exclusionary. The Richmond area was selected because it was accessible to the researcher and included over 1,740 nonprofit organizations of varying sizes and structures (Community Foundation for a Greater Richmond, 2021).

Criteria for inclusion in the study included individuals with at least 3 years of leadership experience in the nonprofit sector. Leadership was defined to include both executive level and mid-level or unit-level roles within their respective organization. Leadership experience was also defined as having responsibility over both strategy and implementation of organizational goals within their respective roles. Three years of experience was relevant for the study as subjects would have perspective within their organizational role both before and during the COVID-19 pandemic.

I used purposive sampling to identify initial subjects for individual interviews. Subjects were solicited using a call for research subjects that was approved by the TCSPP Institutional

Review Board (IRB). Solicitations were distributed through various social and professional networks such as locally focused nonprofit networking groups and professional organizations, as well as LinkedIn. Candidates were asked to complete a brief electronic survey to screen for qualification. The survey asked about the candidate's work experience, current work position, and the size and scope of the nonprofit for which they work. I also used snowball sampling, asking interviewees to identify additional candidates who may be able to serve as participants in the research.

The purpose of this sampling criteria was to provide broad representation of the nonprofit sector leadership within a given geographic area in order to understand the similarities and differences of each leader's individual experiences (Maxwell, 2013). It is worth noting that in a recent survey, the Center for Effective Philanthropy found that of 15,000 nonprofit executive directors in the United States, 60% identify as women and 75% identify as white (Buteau, 2019). In order to ensure a diverse sample, I was sure to include at least one person of color and at least one (additional) person identifying as a man before determining I had reached saturation.

A broad initial sampling goal of 30 individual participants allowed for flexibility within the IRB process while also ensuring the opportunity for saturation (Corbin & Strauss, 2015; Creswell, 2018). This was consistent with other recent research that used a grounded theory method to explore similar topics (Bolden et al., 2020; Gilstrap et al., 2016; Witmer & Mellinger, 2016).

Procedures

To conduct this grounded theory research, I used purposive sampling to identify nonprofit leaders with at least 3 years of experience in their nonprofit roles. Leaders who worked for nonprofit organizations with a budget of at least $500,000 were included in study criteria.

While over 55% of nonprofit organizations have budgets that do not even meet the threshold for IRS reporting (National Council of Nonprofits, 2019), an organization with a budget of this size represented approximately 12% of the nonprofit sector and included more organizations likely to have paid full-time staff (as opposed to a volunteer board or staff) implementing its mission and vision. Organizations were not restricted by sector or type. I used an electronic screener survey to identify whether potential participants met the criteria for inclusion in the study (see Appendix A for screener questions). A noted limitation of the study was that even though organizations with budgets of at least $500,000 were eligible for inclusion, only leaders working for organizations with budgets over $1million ended up in the final study as participants.

I conducted semistructured interviews with individuals who met criteria for participation in the study. All interviews were audio and/or video recorded for later transcription. See Appendix B for interview questions.

As interviews were completed and transcribed, I began to code and analyze the interviews for themes (see Data Processing section for additional details). During the analysis process, I looked for opportunities to conduct member checks, returning to individual interviewees to verify or clarify excerpts from their transcripts. However, I did not ultimately need to return to any interviewees for member checking after the initial interview.

Validity

One particular threat to validity in this study was the personal bias I brought to this research. As someone who has worked in the nonprofit field for over 20 years (virtually my entire career), I brought my own experiences and thoughts regarding effective or ineffective leadership and organizational management. I was also biased in my experience of working primarily with nonprofit organizations that serve people in the areas of healthcare and education.

Since the nonprofit arena is vast and diverse, it was important to keep these biases in mind as I conducted interviews and analyzed the produced transcripts. I managed this bias through active journaling.

A similar threat to validity, due to my familiarity with the field and the topic, was making sure that I actively challenged any assumptions that I had regarding the role of ambidexterity in a leader's style or strategy. I needed to keep this in check by keeping an open mind during interviews, making sure I did not ask leading questions, and actively challenging my assumptions through journaling and member checking.

Finally, another threat to validity was ensuring that I collected enough information to achieve saturation in answering my research questions by interviewing an adequate number of participants. I achieved this by canvassing for as broad a sample as possible and checking for saturation through the iterative coding process (Corbin & Strauss, 2015). After five interviews had been completed an abductive process was employed, using a combination of matching interview statements to pre-existing codes while also generating new codes or categories through reviews of the collected data. By interviews 9 and 10, more than 90% of excerpts were able to be coded to existing data, demonstrating saturation.

Instrumentation

As a qualitative, grounded theory study, the primary instrumentation for this research was open-ended questions, delivered via individual, semistructured interviews (see Appendix B for a list of questions). These interviews were held using a teleconference platform (Zoom). All interviews were audio and video recorded for later transcription.

Prior to conducting the individual interviews, all potential participants completed a survey (created using Microsoft Forms). The survey asked questions regarding inclusion criteria, including whether the participant worked for a nonprofit organization, the organization's size and industry focus, their role within the organization, and their years of experience within a leadership position (see Appendix A for screening survey questions). Once the participants were identified as meeting screening requirements and provided consent to participate in research, interviews were scheduled and conducted.

A transcript of the interview was created automatically using the Zoom platform from the recording. This transcript was hand-checked against the recording for accuracy. To ensure validity, I had the ability to use member checking to take excerpts of the interview back to study participants to verify the content; however, this did not turn out to be necessary. I also utilized memoing to document thoughts and notes and process my bias throughout the entire research study, including during the conduction of interviews and periods of data analysis.

Data Processing

A grounded theory approach involves the transcription and subsequent analysis of all interviews (Corbin & Strauss, 2015). All interviews were transcribed manually. Then the transcriptions were analyzed, first using line-by-line analysis, and then using an iterative process that supported identification of axial codes and categories (Corbin & Strauss, 2015; Saldana, 2021). After the first five interviews had been completed, I started focused coding, grouping individual codes with similar topics or meanings. This began an abductive process, using a combination of matching interview statements to pre-existing codes and generating new codes or categories through reviews of the collected data. By interviews 9 and 10, more than 90% of excerpts were able to be coded to existing data. At this point, I began to consider that saturation had been established (Corbin & Strauss, 2015; Hallberg, 2009). Across the 10 interviews, 878 individual codes were generated and were applied to 2094 excerpts. There was an average of 209.4 codes per interview (range = 169-331).

The next step in the process was to categorize the focused codes, creating a qualitative codebook which enabled the development of emerging categories and themes. Statements from each interview were coded to these themes (Saldana, 2021). A random sample of one interview was cross-checked by a colleague to validate coding. Inter-coding reliability was over 80%. Then, the axial codes and categories were further analyzed for themes. These themes provided the foundation for the grounded theory that emerged from the data (Hunter et al., 2011).

Assumptions

There were three key assumptions regarding this research. The first was that the subjects participating in interviews would answer honestly and reflectively regarding their own experiences. Another assumption was that participants would share this information willingly, having provided formal consent. Further, their selection for participation outside of any formal relationship with the researcher minimized the possibility of coercion or biased influence. A third key assumption was that a qualitative approach, specifically the use of grounded theory, was the most appropriate method for exploring the research questions under investigation. Seeking to understand the application of a complex, collaborative leadership style that has been relatively unexplored in a nonprofit context is best researched through a method that employs a grounded theory approach.

Limitations

A noted limitation in the design of this study was that it was impossible to include nonprofit leaders from every size or type of nonprofit organization. The nature of a qualitative study includes relatively small sample sizes, which inherently limited the quantity of data I could expect to collect for analysis (Creswell, 2018). Aiming for a broad sample and interviewing subjects until saturation had been reached mitigated this challenge. Additionally, collecting information from leaders representing multiple levels of an organization supported broad coverage of the research questions under investigation.

Another limitation was the role that my bias as a person who has worked in the nonprofit field for the bulk of my career brought to the research. While a grounded theory approach employed a process of comparison to existing knowledge and discovered themes through the interview and analysis process, it was incumbent on me as a researcher to keep my own biases in mind as I explored these themes for the purposes of understanding (Charmaz & Belgrave, 2012). This limitation was mitigated through memoing and member checking during both the interview and analysis processes.

Ethical Assurances

In order to ensure ethical protection of participants, multiple procedures were followed. Although some study participants were acquaintances or professional colleagues, none of the participants were closely associated with me, either as a family relative or current or past close business associate (e.g., customer, supervisor, supervisee, etc.) The study received approval from the TCSPP Institutional Review Board (IRB) prior to the recruitment of any subjects or interview completion. All participants read the consent form and provided their consent through the process approved by the IRB (see Appendix C).

The participation of all research subjects was confidential. Interviews were recorded and stored on a secure, password-encrypted platform that was accessible only to me. Once interviews were transcribed and checked, original recordings were destroyed. Each participant was assigned a pseudonym and was identified in transcripts and reporting of research only through that false name. Any other possible identifying information, including the names of organizations, coworkers, etc. was redacted or otherwise masked when results were reported. A separate document that included a cross-reference of identifying information and used pseudonyms was stored in a secure location for my reference if needed. Any transcriptions (with identifying information redacted) were stored on a secure, password-encrypted platform (digitally) or in a locked file cabinet accessible only to me (if paper copies were needed). These files will be stored for 5 years, in accordance with American Psychological Association (APA) guidelines. After that time, transcripts will be destroyed securely (shredded and/or erased).

Summary

This study explored how nonprofit leaders use ambidextrous leadership practices to support their organization's unique needs for innovation and production. A Straussian grounded theory approach was used because it aligned with my epistemology of pragmatism and critical realism. Moreover, a grounded theory approach supported the exploration of a process over a quantitative examination of direct cause and effect (Maxwell, 2013).

Gaining a greater understanding of the specific behaviors utilized by nonprofit leaders in real-world contexts can be accomplished through a grounded theory approach (Hunter et al., 2011). Additionally, the grounded theory approach acknowledges the role that previous history, the researcher's own experience and bias, and the general role that subjectivity plays in the exploration of the research questions (Charmaz, 2014).

In conducting this study, I used purposive sampling to identify 10 nonprofit leaders who had at least 3 years of leadership or management experience in their respective roles. Participants completed individual semistructured interviews. Transcripts of recorded interviews were analyzed using an iterative coding process to identify themes (Corbin & Strauss, 2015).

Techniques such as memoing and inter-rater coding were used to minimize bias and support research validity.

To ensure ethical research practices, the study received approval through the TCSPP Institutional Review Board (IRB) and all participants provided written consent before data was collected. All potentially identifying participant data remained confidential and was stored in a secure fashion.

Chapter 4: Findings

Introduction

The purpose of this study was to understand the skills and knowledge that nonprofit leaders utilize to implement ambidextrous leadership practices within their respective organizations. Ambidextrous leadership is generally defined as a flexible response to situational factors in order to facilitate maximal opportunities within the organization for innovation or production (Sun et al., 2020). As nonprofit leaders are called to balance current capacity with the need to drive their mission, the use of ambidextrous leadership is vital to success (Zhang et al., 2017).

The specific research question under exploration was how do nonprofit leaders use ambidextrous leadership practices to support their organization's unique needs for innovation and production? Under this broad question, I explored three specific subquestions. These were:

1. How do nonprofit leaders use elements of ambidextrous leadership to collaborate with other organizations or utilize a shared leadership model?

2. What elements of ambidextrous leadership are most supportive to a nonprofit organization's need for innovation?

3. What elements of ambidextrous leadership are most supportive to a nonprofit organization's need for production?

These research questions were explored using a qualitative grounded theory research approach that included individual semistructured interviews. These interviews were analyzed for categories and themes.

Study Participants

Once approval to begin research had been received from the TCSPP IRB, a solicitation for participants was shared in multiple ways. I shared IRB-approved study solicitations on my personal LinkedIn and Facebook pages and was given permission to share the solicitations with two nonprofit-based groups; one was a professional organization and the other was an informal networking group of nonprofit leaders. Study participants also received the solicitation through snowball sampling (friends of colleagues or study participants). All potential participants were directed to an online survey that included the screener survey and consent form. If participants provided consent, additional demographics and contact information were collected. Then, I contacted survey respondents to schedule individual interviews at a mutually convenient time. Interviews were conducted between June and September 2022.

Demographics

A total of 18 participants completed the screener survey. Of that number, four did not meet screener criteria and one did not consent to participate in the research process. Of the remaining 13 qualified candidates, three were unable to schedule individual interviews. A total of 10 participants completed individual semistructured interviews. Seventy percent (70%) of the participants identified as women and 30% identified as men. Eighty percent (80%) identified as White/Caucasian while one participant (10%) identified as Hispanic/Latino and one participant (10%) identified as multiple race. This was somewhat aligned with national research. The Center for Effective Philanthropy noted in a recent survey of nonprofit leaders that approximately 60% identify as female and 75% identify as white (Buteau, 2019). Since this was a qualitative study, true demographic representation alignment to the population was not a requirement; however, these data support my interest to achieve transparency and trust.

These participants represented community organizations that varied in size and scope. Seventy percent (70%) had budgets of over $5 million and 30% had budgets of $1-4.9 million. While leaders representing organizations with budgets of $500,000 to just under $1 million qualified for the study, none were identified to participate. Half of the organizations represented (50%) served in the human services sector. Twenty percent (20%) were affiliated with healthcare organizations and 30% of the leaders served in education or research organizations. Table 3 provides a visual summary of the general participant profiles. Figures 5 and 6 provide a visual summary of individual participant demographics and organizational demographics.

Table 3

Participant Profile

Participant	Race	Gender	Organization Size ($$)	Service Sector
P1	White	Woman	$5 million+	Human Services
P2	White	Woman	$1-4.9 million	Healthcare
P3	White	Woman	$1-4.9 million	Human Services
P4	Multiple Race	Woman	$5 million+	Education/Research
P5	White	Woman	$5 million+	Education/Research
P6	Hispanic/Latino	Woman	$1-4.9 million	Human Services
P7	White	Man	$5 million+	Education/Research
P8	White	Woman	$5 million+	Healthcare
P9	White	Man	$5 million+	Human Services
P10	White	Man	$5 million+	Human Services

Figure 5

Participant Demographics Summary

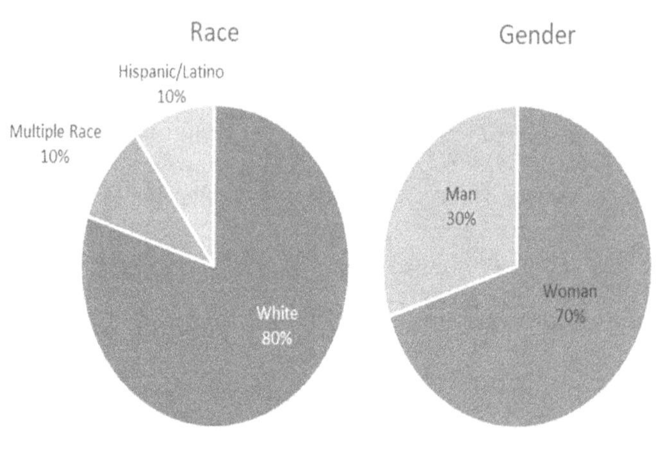

Figure 6

Organization Demographics Summary

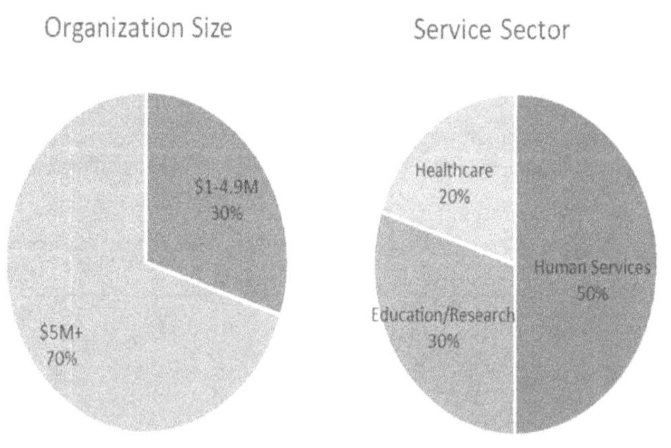

Results

Grounded theory is a systematic qualitative methodology that uses a constant

comparative method to gain understanding and knowledge around a social science phenomenon

(Hallberg, 2009). The Straussian approach acknowledges that both previous knowledge of the

researcher and existing research play a critical role in the process of coding, understanding, and

categorizes information gleaned from qualitative, semistructured interviews and other relevant

data (Hunter et al., 2011). As mentioned previously, Glaser's Six C's framework supports the

researcher by providing a positivist-leaning structure to a qualitative methodology (Glaser,

1978). It considers the relationship between Causes, Contexts, Contingencies, Consequences,

Covariances, and Conditions with respect to a core category (or behavior under investigation)

(see Figure 1). The core category emerging from the constant comparative method of data

analysis is the primary focal point of a research question guided by a grounded theory approach

(Hallberg, 2009).

The Core Category

In this study, joint space emerged as the primary engine that answers the question: How

do nonprofit leaders use the principles of ambidextrous leadership to support their unique needs

of innovation and production? In multiple interviews, leaders shared how they engaged in

specific behaviors that supported their aims towards innovation and production for their

respective organizations. These behaviors shared two key characteristics: they often included

individual behaviors that occurred in a cycle over time and they typically happened via

collaboration (with external organizations) or using a shared leadership framework (within the

organization).

The processes for achieving innovation and production are similar but do share some key differences (see Figure 7). The innovation process includes researching, creating a vision, crafting a road map, communicating a plan and getting feedback from others, and then initiating the plan through a process that often includes multiple attempts or trial and error (adjust and regroup). The production process also includes a space for research and communication within the cycle. However, one way the engagement process within the production cycle differs from that in the innovation cycle is that the leader focuses on utilization of a problem solving process and refinement of current work instead of visioning and the definition of a road map. An assessment of priorities also comes into play during the production process.

Figure 7

Innovation and Production Cycles

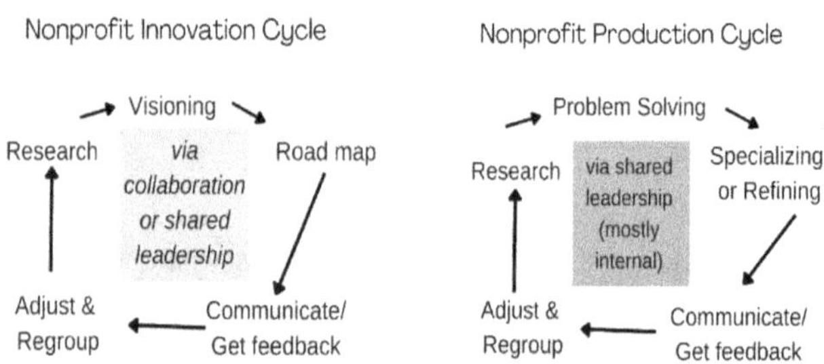

Breaking down the elements of these cycles, I saw categorical codes emerge from multiple interview respondents, demonstrating not only the presence of each behavior across multiple leaders, but the role that collaboration or shared leadership played in each as well.

Research (Innovation and Production)

Research is a key element of both the innovation and productivity process. Multiple interviews related activities such as feasibility research, reading articles on trends and current events, and gathering data to support the need for ideas. These are typically done independently

but then this research is subsequently shared with team members or collaborators.

> [for innovation] So I'm saying tell me why this is a bad idea, tell me everything…wrong
>
> with this and…how this is going to fit in your workflow because really it could be the
>
> best tech in the world, but if…you don't see benefit in it, then there's no need for us to do
>
> it. (P1)
>
> [for production] It's usually a group. I usually do the research piece, you know, this is
>
> what…we can do, and I take that back and typically [meet with directors about it]. (P5)

One thing that stands out as a difference between the innovation and productivity cycles

is the step after research. In innovation, this was seen as visioning, leading to development of a

road map; however, in productivity, it was often seen as problem solving, which led to

refinement or specialization. P9 expressed insight about the difference between the two:

> Now my VP…and I are having a conversation about strategy as opposed to problem
>
> solving. So, we introduced this concept to our team a couple weeks ago. The difference
>
> between leadership and management is to say that problem-solving is important…but
>
> …it's an influence model [based on] self-awareness. What do you need to do to get there?
>
> And then [what is] your ability to influence others? That's leadership. And if we stay in
>
> this problem-solving place, then we're not going to get to innovation.

Visioning (Innovation)

The visioning process can occur as a solitary activity as well; however, this is more often

seen as a brainstorming process within a group of colleagues. Words and phrases used by

interview participants such as "think differently", "use my time to play things out", "idea

generation", and "put my thinking cap on" characterize this work.

> We're only going to talk about things we could potentially give you that are new. What
> are we not doing that we should be? (P9)

> [Our CEO] is gifted at vision and advocacy and she hasn't been able to do a lot of that
> because she's been intensely focused in the programs. (P6)

Road Map (Innovation)

After the vision has been crafted and honed, the next stage of innovation involves crafting a road map. Interviewees mentioned specific tactics such as developing a timeline or asking the question, "How do we get there?"

> When you're talking about something larger like what we're working on right now, there
> are a lot of meetings going on to determine what that roadmap is going to be first and
> then, once we have a roadmap, then we can get our timeline better identified. (P5)

Problem Solving (Production)

On the productivity side, after a period of research, leaders jump instead to a problem-solving space. This could be done within a group (similar to visioning) and may even include utilization of a consultant or someone with subject matter expertise to hone in on the challenges and solutions needed. The problem solving process can also involve troubleshooting or seeking feedback from team members or collaborators to refine the need.

> [We] bring in a developer who's going to be part of that process and then just sharing
> with them, okay we've found this solution that will help make [our] life, a little bit easier.
> Are you interested in implementing this? (P5)

> Our partner capacity and capability development, that is all…anchored in real
> relationship development, and that will follow…a cadence that is…individualized to the

partnerships...The individuals within these organizations are down to business [to solve problems]. (P10)

Specializing (Production)

The specialization process flows from problem solving in the productivity space. This often plays out by honing the roles of individuals within the group, based on their expertise. During this part of the process, understanding who can best support the need and assigning job roles for the next step are key parts to the process.

They know they're part of the overall. That's why I kind of look at the overall team contribution versus (and as well as) individual contribution. Or if somebody's left behind...but so-and-so brought in an extra [something]. So, they do a part of it. (P7)

Communication and Feedback (Innovation and Production)

After creating a road map or specialization, the next step involves communicating the plan to the greater group and gathering feedback. This could be within the organization, within or across teams. It could also be across organizations through a collaborative process. Many leaders shared their role in this process was to ask opinions, solicit feedback, and reach out to make sure stakeholders were included in the implementation process.

[for innovation] And even though you should be the decision maker...if your board or somebody [is] saying this...you have to go with what your board is saying. But I like to let them know how I stand. (P2)

[for production] If I didn't know how to do something I either called somebody who was in that role or was a peer of mine and say, "Hey listen, I've got this problem or challenge...I'm not sure how to do this. What do you recommend?" (P2)

Adjust and Regroup (Innovation and Production)

The result of reaching out and communicating or soliciting feedback is that the road map or plan frequently requires adjustment. The next step in the process is to adjust and regroup. This may involve realigning timelines because of situational needs, finding additional people to support the challenge at hand, or even using a "trial and error" process to pilot new endeavors. All of this may lead the team back to more research, either to refine the current innovation or efficiency, or to move forward to the next big project.

[for innovation] If you try some things that didn't work well…you realize you don't do it again, but… sometimes it's just trial and error. I mean, you don't know if it's gonna work or not till you do it. (P2)

[for production] But generally we have unpredicted crisis all the time, and crisis is a strong word, but something always is broken that needs to be fixed. (P9)

[We had] this new person who was particularly savvy with databases who I had worked with previously, and I said, "This is a project I want you to solve it." I was like. I know we can do better. (P8)

I never have enough time to do everything…but I have probably the tools to be productive. (P4)

Innovation Using the Six C's Model

As you zoom out from the core category of the innovation and productivity behaviors demonstrated in cycle by nonprofit leaders, the elements of the Six C's Model provide a helpful framework for structuring additional categories that emerged from the data (see Figure 8 for a visual model). The <u>consequence</u> of these core behaviors is innovation, or the new ideas or programs implemented by the organization to accomplish its mission.

The <u>context</u> that frames innovation speaks specifically to a culture or mindset towards innovation. This can be fostered or promoted directly by the leader, but in the larger picture of organizational culture, it is often larger than the leader themselves. Shared examples of a mindset towards innovation included giving permission to innovate, supporting a culture of continuous improvement, pushing boundaries, and scaling existing frameworks. For example, "Innovation is part of everything that I'm doing" (P7). "Are we going to create the structure that supports managed risk and successful innovation (P10)?" "Just because it's hard doesn't mean you shouldn't do it, right? (P1)"

The <u>cause</u> can be seen as the leader and stakeholder capabilities. This specifically speaks to their individual focus towards innovation in their work and their personality orientation. For example, P6 shared, "[My CEO] being able to trust me…with programs has…opened up some space for her to think about, okay, now I can kind of do this over here." Also, P4 shared, "I'm from the school where my focus is…if you don't ask for [it] right away [you will] start off not getting it."

The <u>conditions</u> involve having the right resources. Interviewees shared examples that included human resources, financial capital, and supplies or institutional knowledge to accomplish the work. When describing needs for a new project, P5 shared:

We never had a project manager on our team, and so the analysts acted as project managers of our small little projects; but we knew if this was going to be a huge 5-year project that we were going to need a project manager on the team. Similarly, P3 shared, "This year we got a new program approved that never launched…because we didn't have the staff stability to do it."

Figure 8

Visual Model of Innovation

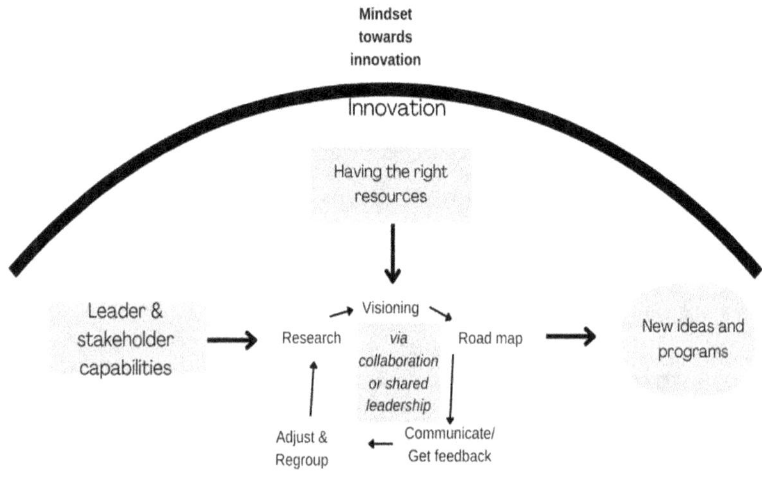

Production Using the Six C's Model

A similar model with somewhat different elements can be seen for production. The consequence of these core behaviors is improved production or efficiency within the organization (see Figure 9 for a visual model)

The context that frames productivity is also reflective of culture. The theme that resonated here was one of a coaching or learning mindset. Again, this was fostered or promoted directly by the leader, but was also seen in the larger picture of organizational culture. Shared examples of a mindset towards coaching and learning included developing leader skill sets, having a strong work ethic, and an organizational culture that promoted efficiency or playing multiple roles. For example, in assessing the needs of her team members, P6 shared:

> So, I'm not going to judge you based on what you did today. But, you know, I'm going to look at the whole week, and when we meet weekly…we're going to talk about what [happened]. You know, did you have a bad day?

When speaking about work ethic, P2 shared, "I think that's just something…it's an inside sort of thing or you're brought up with or that's just me, because I know some people [who] are like, 'Nope! Done!'"

In contrast to the <u>cause</u> of innovation behaviors, causes of production behaviors extended to the role of an organization's structure, training opportunities, and a leader orientation focused on task orientation and being very organized. As an example of leader orientation, P4 said, "I'm just super organized," and P2 described herself as "I've been told I get it done faster than the average person."

An example of organization structure came from P3 with "[We put] high resource [where more] resources needed, and the higher the risk, then the more formal [the process] became." Similarly, with the importance of training and written procedures, P4 shared:

I've gotten push back from folks about [formal training]. [They say] that's not the only way to [do that]. You don't have to write everything out…but if you decide to win the lottery and leave in a week, you know, I'm still trying to figure out how you did it.

A prominent category for <u>conditions</u> that emerged in all interviews around productivity was the use of metrics to find efficiencies. P10 shared, "There is…a continuum of tactics you can employ to develop and track productivity and efficiency depending on the nature of the work and operations." Similarly, when speaking of the difference between innovation and production behaviors, P7 shared, "I think the only difference is…our outcomes…and how we're going to be measured." Participant 1 also related the importance of metrics by saying, "You know, are we meeting certain productivity expectations? Because we have expectations on us from the staff."

Figure 9

Visual Model of Production

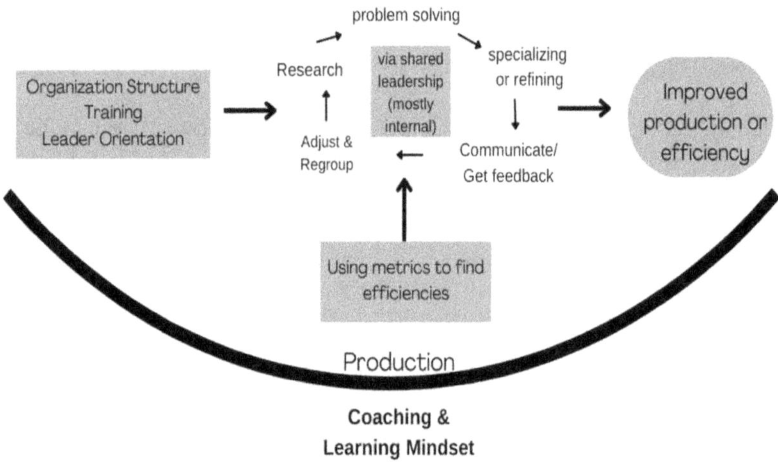

The Role of Barriers and Contingencies

Leaders were able to share in their individual interviews both barriers and contingencies

that impacted the innovation or productivity processes. These can be seen as <u>covariances</u> within

the Six C's Model. Barriers are elements that can slow down or stagnate either process while

contingencies are leader traits or behaviors that facilitate the overall use of ambidexterity (see

Figure 10 for a visual model).

Some barriers impacted causes. For example, having the wrong stakeholders at the table

for a conversation, a values mismatch between collaborators and stakeholders, or having the

wrong "person fit" for the role all impacted the process with respect to capabilities or leader

orientation. Other barriers were seen to specifically impact conditions. For instance, gaps in

capacity or safety and security issues could impact resource assessment and use on both the

productivity and innovation sides. Communication challenges were also cited as frequent barriers

and this impacted the core innovation and productivity cycles that ultimately led to an innovation or improved efficiency. P5 recounted a barrier on a new project, "The unions were on board with it, everybody was on board with that, and then all of a sudden security got word of it and said no, not happening. So yeah it's not identifying the right stakeholders and a lack of communication." Another example from P4:

> If you work with someone who is really kind of used to being in their own silo and saying, you know it's due the 30th, but you know I'll get your draft by the 15th…and then it's the first and [you have nothing]. So those are stressful type of relationships, where you know there's definitely two different styles that are working together and the bottom line is it gets done but it's still stressful.

Leaders shared many examples of traits, attitudes, and behaviors that facilitated the use of ambidexterity, or that continual shifting between competing priorities and needs within the organization across time. These included viewing the balance between innovation and production as a constant process, making time to reflect on changes over time, and setting aside time to prioritize innovation, collaboration, and idea generation. Additional contingencies included using active listening, utilizing situational awareness to stay attuned to organizational needs, and engaging in strategic planning on a regular basis to assess needs and priorities. A final key category that emerged as a contingency was engaging in or promoting activities that supported the leader themselves or members of their teams to maintain a healthy balance between life and work and to support the individual needs of employees (and themselves). When talking about the use of strategic planning in his work, P10 said, "We're getting people kind of reflecting on where we are, what's going on, and what's working, and what isn't and reflecting on what may need to happen in the future, just to sort of signal to everyone." In talking about supporting others and self, P6 said:

They're not focused on…solely focused on survival and just…the next thing. They're also

thinking about what can I do to change or what is missing. I think there's a safety. There's

almost like they're feeling really safe with me and with the organization as a whole. That

now they're opening, kind of, those channels for dreaming and I'm right there, like, yes!

Figure 10

Visual Model of Barriers and Contingencies

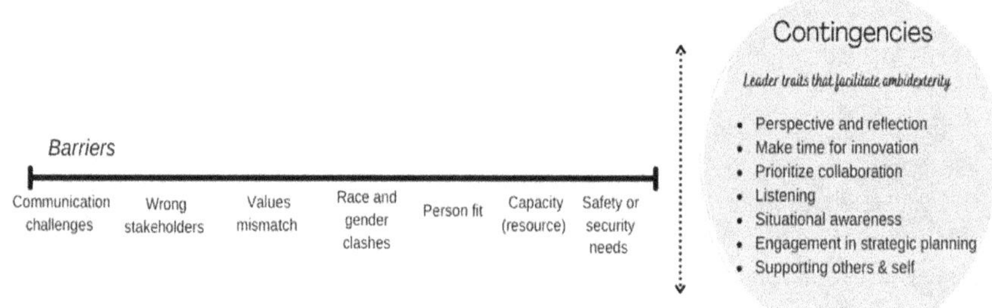

Interaction Between Innovation and Productivity

What emerged from the process of thinking about the categorized data within a Six C's

Model was two separate but inter-related cycles that leaders utilize in their ongoing work with

their respective organizations. Nonprofit leaders can find themselves involved in either the

innovation or production cycle at given points in time. This is shaped by organizational needs as

well as the barriers and contingencies influencing their work. The full framework is seen as a

constant flow back and forth over time (see Figure 11 for the full model).

It's definitely a circle. Because you know, innovation isn't limited to novel strategies or

interventions, right? And so…we take something through an inefficient cycle or a cycle

of inefficiency, as we're learning. And then we're applying systems to that intervention

that improve that. Systematize and operationalize and develop, you know, standards of performance. And then we're running that through our operations. And then we make

observations, and we're evaluating, and we may be able to make modifications to what

we're doing while continuing to operate it. (P10)

Figure 11

Innovation and Production Models in Context

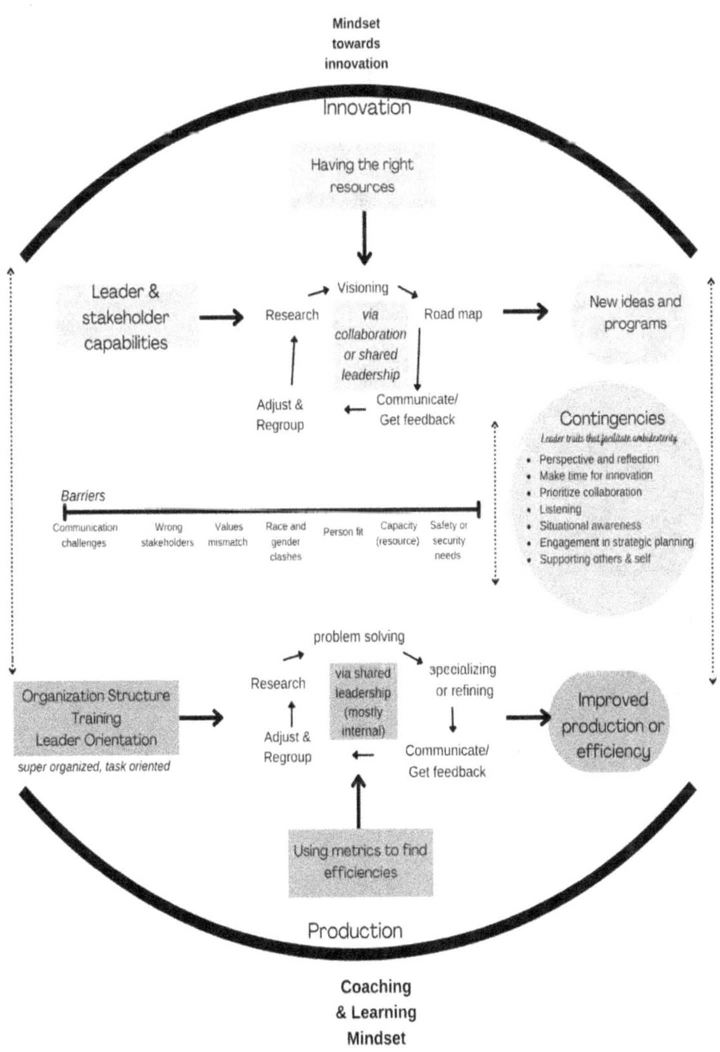

The Nature of Joint space

Collaboration and shared leadership play important roles in the function and success of nonprofit organizations. The interplay of nonprofit leaders with internal and external stakeholders is vital to organizational success (Mathews, 2020; Shier & Handy, 2020). Further, a shared leadership model has been identified as a key factor to organizational resilience and adaptability (Routhieaux, 2015).

Previous studies have defined shared leadership as internal organizational work that distributes leadership opportunities across employees (Routhieaux, 2015). This sits in contrast to organizations where a small group of leaders direct with broad executive power. Existing research largely looks at shared leadership within team settings and is largely defined by interdependence within teams (Freund, 2018; Routhieaux, 2015; Wu et al., 2020). Collaboration, on the other hand, generally refers to work across organizations or agencies (Bryson et al., 2015). The term is sometimes used interchangeably with partnerships, particularly in the nonprofit sector.

For the purposes of this research, collaboration generally refers to leader interactions with stakeholders outside the organization (aligned agencies, individuals served, etc.) while shared leadership is reflective of internal work between different departments or teams within the organization. For ease of reporting in this section, when results apply to both collaboration and shared leadership, I will use the term "joint space."

Information collected from research participants confirmed the strong role that joint space plays in fostering ambidextrous leadership behaviors within nonprofit organizations. Innovation behaviors were shaped by both collaboration and shared leadership while production behaviors were more frequently observed in a shared leadership context (internal to the organization only; see Figure 11).

Breaking the role of joint space down further, categories emerged in the data that supported why leaders engage in these joint space behaviors, the leader's perception of their role in joint space, and specific tactics that leaders use to engage in joint space (see Figure 12).

Why do Leaders Engage in Joint Space?

An overwhelming motivator for engagement in collaboration is that joint priorities overlap between the leader's organization and that of their partners. Additional motivating factors include cost sharing opportunities, feasibility for program replication, and an opportunity to try something new (innovation). "It's almost like the lines have become blurred between them as an organization and us as an organization," said P6 about a particularly successful collaboration. P2 similarly shared, "You just know what each person is doing or talking about." Also, P10 recounted, "It's also fostered and reinforced by being very intentional about the agreements we make with our national organization and with [other organizations]."

The motivation for shared leadership work within the organization is primarily what many interviewees referred to as "breaking down silos." This was a common theme that was brought forward by many participants. An additional motivator for shared leadership is the opportunity it provides for different perspectives and increased diversity at multiple leadership levels. P5 shared, "It's a constant collaboration." P10 described it as "the flow of communication at all levels within the organization and [finding] ways that we can work together to be more effective and efficient." In describing her colleagues, P4 said, "People are used to being in silos," but then shared, "Some folks are more like 'let me figure it out myself' but I think you don't."

What Does the Leader See as Their Role in Joint Space?

When engaging with outside organizations, the interviewed participants often see their role as that of a facilitator. They shared examples that included educating others, listening, and using collaboration as an opportunity to share stories or network with similarly-minded professionals. The leader role in an internal capacity (shared leadership) took on the flavor of guide and coach. They saw their role as a place to influence but not micromanage; they were mindful to act slowly and to be open about growth when engaging in shared leadership opportunities. At least half of the participants (P1, P3, P4, P5, P7) recounted examples of being approached by outside organizations or groups to facilitate collaboration opportunities. Speaking of one experience, P7 said, "We ended up discovering a lot of great information, and having great conversation, because we were able to probably include several people that we were not previously able to include." Internally, this was also shared broadly. P9 said, "We have to have the guts to talk as a team about tough things." Talking about the use of a shared leadership model in his organization, P7 said, "We wouldn't be as successful as we are if we didn't have it." Each of these roles also aligns with and echoes the innovation and production contexts of having mindsets towards innovation and coaching/learning (respectively; see Figure 11).

How Do Leaders Engage in Joint Space?

In answering this question, there is alignment again between the leader's role and the overall context of the model. Leaders engage in collaboration by primarily using a learning mindset, facilitating interactions between groups using technology, engaging in research to better understand opportunities and needs, and maximizing maturing relationships with other organizations. In the shared leadership space, this occurs through a coordination of effort. Leaders work purposefully to find joint space. Examples include using decision-making processes that operate on consensus, having frequent communications with team members, and developing keen situational awareness. P3 shared that decision-making authority "wasn't officially consensus" in their organization but was close to it. Similarly, P10 said, "In all departments or most departments there are decisions that we make together at the table, and we basically arrive at a consensus decision." P9 also shares, "There are still times where people just want me to make a decision [even when you are] just as collaborative as you can be."

Challenges to Joint Space

Another category that emerged from the data included the challenges that impacted or informed leaders as they engaged in these joint space efforts. The most prevalent challenges were getting the right people at the table and working through big problems. P3 described a challenging collaboration by saying, "The most challenging part was a lack of community will." P1 also recounted the overwhelming challenge of taking on large social problems:

> I think the hardest part has been keeping it small enough to be accomplishable. Right, so people are excited about this, so…we need to bring this group in or we need to get this group in and, hey, let's solve for this, and you know people are really excited because it's such a hot topic and it's such a high priority. And right now, to be honest, there are people who are willing to throw lots of money at kind of solving this process, but for me it's just, you know, as kind of leading the effort, it's really…Yes, we want to solve the big picture, but we're not going to be able to do that. What we can do is, let's chunk it, let's break it into accomplishable chunks and keep the group small so that we can actually get the work done.

Other challenges mentioned included having difficult conversations, persevering through crisis, finding the time for group collaboration or engagement, and progress stalling due to external factors. P6 shared, "Collaboration with [OrgX], we've had to have some difficult conversations with them about, you know, this is how our partnership needs to work in order for us to continue." Speaking of a challenge with collaboration, P5 said, "You only get together three times a year and that's it." These challenges are reflective of research by Tsasis (2009) that concluded, "A central challenge for organizations is to manage their boundaries with other organizations" (p. 6).

Figure 12

Utilization of Joint space in Ambidexterity Models (for Nonprofit Leaders)

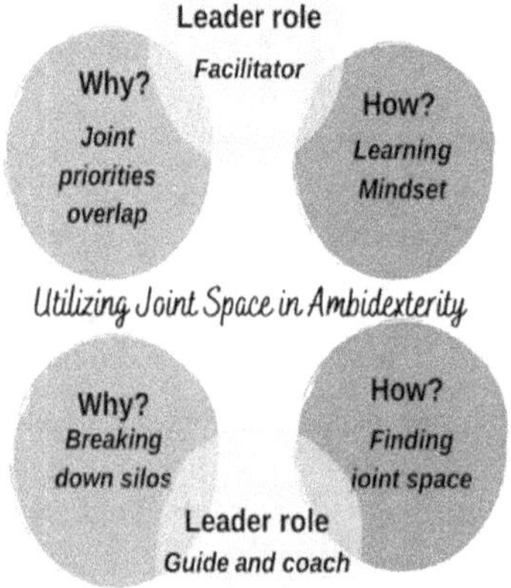

Other Findings

Outside of the core research questions, some additional findings were revealed that are relevant to nonprofit leadership. In the following section, I will share data that emerged surrounding both the impact of the COVID-19 pandemic on leadership behaviors and information gained around why nonprofit leadership may be different from leadership in the for-

profit sector.

The Impact of COVID-19

One area that was explored through the individual interviews was the leader's perceptions

of the impact of the COVID-19 pandemic on their leadership style and behaviors. As a recent

global crisis, COVID-19 had a universal impact on many aspects of life and work and served as a

common focal point for the discussion of crisis and situational needs from an organizational

perspective. Previous research and the original conceptual framework for this study confirm the

role that crisis plays in influencing leadership behaviors (Fazzi & Zamaro, 2016; Gilstrap et al.,

2016; Judge & Piccolo, 2004; see Figure 2).

Every leader interviewed reflected that COVID-19 had impacted their work and

leadership behavior within their respective organization. "It found the weak spots," recounted

P3. A common theme that emerged with the role that emotion played in adjusting leadership

decisions. "I came up with a more team-based way of getting our work done," reflected P9.

Leaders universally understood that they needed to let things go. "I couldn't do it all,"

reflected P3. Re-evaluating needs due to time and other resource capacities was a behavior

shared by many leaders. In particular, understanding that metrics for evaluation needed to be

reconsidered or even placed on hold for a period of time due to their relevancy was a common

theme. "The reality is that personal and professional lives were way more blurred than before the

pandemic," said P10. "The metrics we used in a normal time just didn't apply in this time period

and I had to let that go," shared P6.

Another adjustment for leaders was in their decision-making processes. Some leaders

expressed an overwhelming sense of decision overload. There was no time to think or documentation felt oppressive. Other leaders reflected on their need to be more decisive in their role as a leader. Having been used to a consensus governance model, conditions created by the COVID-19 pandemic forced more unilateral decision making on the part of executive leaders (even if temporarily) and this was a significant style shift for some individuals. "The number one change right out of the gate, so I had to alter my style to be. I had to be a decider. I wasn't able, and it wasn't feasible to just be collaborative." (P9)

All leaders reflected on adjustments that had to be made in communication style and methods. Leaders needed to clarify more often, provide more intentional feedback, and assess individual team members' accessibility. Some adjustments, such as the opportunity for virtual meetings, brought convenience and a new way of doing business that has supported leaders and their respective organizations even as the pandemic has waned and businesses are more open to in-person meetings. "I had to be ok with not all my staff being in-person for staff meetings," shared P8 and P6 said, "I had to be a lot more involved with [staff members'] personal lives." Examples of positive perspectives included, "We never did Zoom [before]…but why wouldn't you use Zoom? So, you can see people as much as you possibly can." (P7) and P2 said, "I just think it's more effective for me, working at home."

Overall, many leaders reflected that the COVID-19 pandemic changed their mindset around both leadership and resource management. "It challenged me as a leader," said P1. "It shifted the way we do that business" (P5). As leaders adjusted budgets, spent only what was necessary, and put projects on hold, it forced them to re-evaluate priorities for their organization. From an ambidexterity perspective, many of these shifts could be perceived as productivity or exploitation behaviors rather than innovation behaviors. While new ideas and ways of doing business did emerge during the pandemic, these shifts to optimize resources sit strongly in the productivity space (Havermans et al., 2015).

What Makes the Nonprofit Space Different?

As other research has pointed out, nonprofit organizations face different challenges than organizations in other business sectors (Aboramadan & Kundi, 2020; Bish & Becker, 2016). Further, leadership in the nonprofit space is often under-researched or results of research with for-profit businesses are generally applied to nonprofits without a consideration of differences (Peng, 2019). For this reason, individual interviews with the nonprofit leaders explored this question, asking them to consider what makes leadership in the nonprofit sector different.

Resource scarcity was a common category that emerged from this question. Reflections from multiple interviews captured this, such as: "You have to do the best with what you got" (P6); "It depends on the priorities that the leader is given" (P7); "We had to make sure we weren't doing anything that wasn't necessary." (P5) Competition for resources and resource scarcity were clear dominators of leadership behavior across the board.

Contrastingly, another theme that differentiated nonprofit from its for-profit counterparts was the focus on mission, and specifically a mission for people. "A nonprofit's role," P7 shared, "is to be an agent of change and hope." P3 also said, "Corporate tasks…are often defined by the bottom line. …Whereas in a nonprofit…a lot of [leadership] is driven by [things that] are much more vague and much more hard *(sic)* to measure." Additionally, individuals who had worked in for-profit spaces reflected that there was a common sense of more flexibility, more camaraderie, and more room for negotiation in nonprofit spaces. From an ambidexterity perspective, this is largely reflective of exploration behaviors over exploitation behaviors.

Finally, an interesting category that emerged from this discussion included perspective on a philosophy and approach to business practices. This general category could be broken down into three subcategories. In the first category, leaders acknowledged that a nonprofit is "still a business" and, as such, needed to utilize and practice good business strategy, just like a for-profit enterprise. However, another group of leaders acknowledged that they encountered active resistance and even ambivalence around utilizing these *best business practices* in the nonprofit space. For example, P1 said, "It's been harder as a nonprofit to follow some of the best practices that we see in…private for-profit companies, because our end goal is never supposed to be about profits; but profits still matter and you know that money still matters." P8 added, "I think it's really important for leaders in…nonprofit to learn from the…for-profit sector and gain skills from that area." In the third group, leaders reflected challenges with coworkers or board members who lack financial skills and savvy. P8 later shared:

> In small and medium nonprofits, I would find these wonderfully, beautifully passionate people about their cause. But they don't know how to put a budget together. They don't know how to set goals. They don't know how to determine what their metrics should be, or how to even calculate those metrics…They're so down in the weeds with the mission.

In the long run, many leader reflections around business practices indicate that they understand the need to utilize good business savvy but do not always have the skills, staff strength, or know-how to implement these practices consistently.

Summary

This study sought to examine how nonprofit leaders use ambidextrous leadership practices to support their organization's unique needs for innovation and production. A total of

10 individuals participated in semistructured interviews. These interviews were coded and analyzed for themes using a Straussian grounded theory approach.

Analysis of the data revealed that the core category that answers the primary research question is joint space. Nonprofit leaders engage in cycles of activity that lead to innovation or production. The common element between all leaders is the use of joint space within these cycles, either in collaboration with other organizations (external) or using a shared leadership approach (internal). The process of engaging in behaviors that support innovation or production occurs in a cyclical pattern over time, with leaders adjusting their behaviors based on situational factors. Additional barriers and contingencies respectively impede or facilitate these innovation and production behaviors.

Although not a primary area of interest in this study, additional data revealed the role of crisis in leader behavior through the lens of the COVID-19 pandemic. Leaders reflected on both positive and negative ways that crisis impacted their decision making, management, and communication skills. Another finding from this study was the perception of leaders as to why key leadership skills are (or are not) different for those in the nonprofit sector. Resource scarcity (real or perceived), a focus on mission over profit, and skills and perceptions around fiscal management were primary themes that emerged from the data.

Chapter 5: Summary, Conclusions, and Recommendations

Introduction

The purpose of this qualitative grounded theory study was to understand the skills and knowledge that nonprofit leaders utilize to implement ambidextrous leadership practices within their respective organizations. Ambidexterity is defined as the simultaneous use of exploration and exploitation to pursue a balance of innovation and production (Sun et al., 2020). This balance can occur through shared leadership or through the ambidextrous nature of leaders adapting to environmental variables (Havermans et al., 2015; Uhl-Bien et al., 2007).

While ambidexterity has been studied in many different contexts, the nonprofit sector has explored this subject in a limited way (Aboramadan & Kundi, 2020; Brimhall, 2021). Through interviews with 10 diverse nonprofit leaders, specific behaviors and processes were identified that facilitated innovation and productivity within their respective organizations. A conceptual framework emerged that identified a dynamic process of engagement on the part of the leader in a variety of contexts. This frequently involved engagement in joint space, either through collaboration with external organizations or through an internal shared leadership model.

In this section, I offer reflections, conclusions and recommendations based on the review of literature from chapter two and analysis of collected data in chapter four. Comparisons of the emergent data to existing models, limitations identified through the analysis process, and recommendations for both future research and practitioner utilization will be shared.

Interpretation of Findings

Comparison to Existing Models

Previous research on ambidexterity and complexity endorsed that a combination of innovation (exploration) and production (exploitation) behaviors on the part of leaders results in optimal outcomes for organizations. Uhl-Bien and Arena (2018) demonstrated the fluid nature of innovation, production, and the use of enabling and adaptive space within their conceptual framework for complexity leadership theory. In this way, there are similarities between the conceptual framework identified in this research (see Figure 11) and the Uhl-Bien and Arena model (see Figure 3). What this proposed model adds is further detail on the stages involved in the innovation and production processes, while clarifying the barriers and contingencies involved in the process from the perspective of nonprofit leaders. These barriers and contingencies align with the enabling leadership space in Uhl-Bien and Arena's model.

Uhl-Bien and Arena (2018) also mentioned the role of networks and collaboration in the complexity process. They note that leveraging networks and collaboration to achieve outcomes is essential and that "leaders…need to understand that network features that work at one stage will not work at another" (p. 94). This aligns with the findings in this study around the use of joint space for collaboration with external organizations and shared leadership at an internal level. The stage-based or cyclical nature of the process is similarly aligned, even if not expressly stated within Uhl-Bien and Arena's research.

Uhl-Bien and Arena (2018) used their platform to call for future research, stating that while much of their understanding of complexity leadership is theoretical, the practical implication of organizational adaptability needs further exploration, particularly from a qualitative lens. This work continues to be under-explored in the nonprofit space.

Comparisons and alignment can also be drawn to research by Bish and Becker (2016) and Zimmerman et al. (2018). Both of these studies emphasized the need to find balance in managing tension and the role between top-down versus bottom-up leadership styles. Conclusions reached by both studies that a leader's role may be different both across an organization and within an ambidextrous space aligned with results found through this study as well.

Koster and van Bree (2018) also explored ambidexterity in the nonprofit space. Their work, similarly, identified collaboration as a key component to facilitating ambidexterity. It did not, however, identify specific behaviors or components of that collaboration that facilitated innovation and productivity. The current study provides additional dimensions around leadership behavior, process, and facilitating factors that support an ambidextrous approach to organizational management (see Figure 12).

In their qualitative study, Havermans et al. (2015) identified specific exploration and exploitation behaviors that facilitate an ambidextrous approach (see Table 2); however, their study did not identify a specific conceptual framework or process for how those behaviors interact with one another or how leaders make decisions in their use and selection of specific behaviors at certain times. Instead, it emphasized a need for low complexity behaviors when exploitation (productivity) was required and higher complexity behaviors to pursue exploration (innovation). Further, their research was not specific to the nonprofit space.

Looking at perspectives provided by this study's participants around their pursuit of innovation and productivity, it appears that nonprofit leaders spend a lot of time in what Havermans et al. (2015) would define as the exploration space. Behaviors such as involving others, stimulating personal development, working together (engaging in joint space), and accepting mistakes were frequently mentioned by study participants. Less frequent were mentions of exploitation behaviors such as stopping discussions, enforcing rules, or redirecting efforts. It is also interesting to note that when exploitation behaviors were mentioned, it was often in the context of crisis (specifically in response to COVID-19) while innovation was more active when capacity is not stretched. P1 shared a comment that reflected this:

> To think about what would justify adding one more thing, even if it's innovative and even if it's, you know, going to go to have great return on investment. We have to make sure that we have that in context of what we have to do. That struggle has been real, the past year for sure.

This is certainly an area for future research. It is fair to ask whether the engagement in exploration and exploitation behaviors is just a consistent back and forth process. Perhaps leaders may not immediately identify certain behaviors as specifically occurring in pursuit of goals towards innovation versus production?

Innovation Versus Production

This leads to an important question that emerged from analysis of the data regarding whether it matters if there is a specific aim for innovation or production. Alternately, is it more important to acknowledge the constant flow and movement of the process, as identified in the cyclical nature of both the innovation and production cycles (see Figure 7) and the leader's fluid, dynamic engagement between innovation and production behaviors over time (see Figure 11). Perhaps the most important leader behavior involves their awareness or attunement to their place within the process and the utilization of that awareness in their decision making.

As noted in Figure 10, contingencies that facilitated an ambidextrous approach to the leader's work placed an emphasis on reflection or situational awareness, which also reinforces the fluid nature of a dynamic process that alternates focus between innovation and production over time. It is possible that if leaders were unfamiliar with the theories of ambidextrous approaches but still used or applied these principles on a regular basis in their work, the subtle differences between activities aimed at innovation versus that of production could be easy to miss.

Multiple interviews reflected on minimal difference between innovation and production leadership activities. P3 initially said that the processes involved with innovation and production activities were different but then on reflection said, "Maybe it's not so different," with the process differences lying in priority needs in terms of cost and/or time investment. Another perspective was brought by P9 when citing the differences between leadership and management. Their reflection was that staying in that "problem solving space" is a function of production (and management) but utilizing and developing self-awareness, reflection, and a culture of influence is a function of innovation (or leadership).

The similarities between elements of the innovation and production cycles (see Figure 7) outweigh the small perceived differences between the two. It is possible that the differences between the visioning-road map approach to innovation and the problem solving-refining approach for productivity could be easy to miss if leaders are not reflecting on their work from an ambidextrous lens. However, another question that emerges is whether there is really a difference between innovation and production behaviors. While Havermans et al. (2015) defines innovation and production behaviors with certain characteristics, the perception of these differences is not widely researched or explored. In many ways, the fluid movement between innovation and production is more reflective of the complexity leadership framework (Uhl-Bien & Arena, 2018) and the continual shifts between entrepreneurial leadership (innovation), operational leadership (production), and enabling leadership.

Alternately, it may be fair to wonder whether the question regarding differences between innovation and production behaviors could have been worded a different way to research participants. Could the perceived similarities between the two behaviors come about as a function of the way the question was asked?

Finally, does innovation and productivity really play out differently in the nonprofit space? Multiple interviewees reflected on the need to "build the plane while it is flying" (P6) or "wear many hats" (P4) in their nonprofit role. Indeed, nonprofit leaders are known for being nimble and scrappy in the way they often need to pull resources together to make things happen. Could this blur the lines between innovation and production behaviors for nonprofit leaders? When there is resource scarcity, perhaps the lines get even fuzzier between innovation and productivity: all new things are seen as innovation, even if they lead to efficiency in the long run. This is an area for future research and exploration since there does not appear to be much perspective on this in the literature.

The Role of Contingencies

Leaders cited multiple contingencies that facilitated their use of an ambidextrous style in their work. Primary contingencies included active listening, the use of situational awareness, and mindful engagement in strategic planning. It is worth noting that a strong contingency identified by multiple leaders was the promotion of work-life balance for both themselves and for their coworkers or fellow employees. Work design and work-life balance have been identified as key factors to employee engagement in nonprofit organizations (Nguyen & Pham, 2020).

Driven by mission and passion, sometimes to the detriment of both financial income and work resources, employees in nonprofit organizations are at risk to sacrifice their own mental and physical health for the needs of their organization. In a recent study, Riforgiate and Kramer (2021) identified that new employees may experience conflicting messages between organizational policy and leader execution of work-life balance programs or supports.

Additionally, while diverse teams benefit from multiple perspectives that emerge through collaborative work, this plurality of ideas may create conflicting or contrasting messages that must be considered in order to understand the larger picture within a context of equity. This is often where the enabling leadership space of the complexity leadership model takes on primary importance (Uhl-Bien & Arena, 2018). By embracing the conflicts and paradoxes that emerge from multiple perspectives, leaders can facilitate the emergence of new ideas. Leaders who utilize reflective practices such as the contingencies identified through this study can support worker well-being and overall team functionality (see Figure 10). This idea is reinforced through a recent study by Parrello et al. (2021) that studied the support of education teams in an Italian nonprofit at the height of the COVID-19 pandemic.

The Impact of Crisis

While it was not a central focus of the study, participants were asked to reflect on how their leadership style was impacted or changed by the COVID-19 pandemic. Previous research identified that crisis is a factor in decision-making capabilities for nonprofit leaders (Fazzi & Zamaro, 2016; Gilstrap et al., 2016; Judge & Piccolo, 2004). Study participants reinforced the impact that a global crisis such as the COVID-19 pandemic had on their communication styles, flexibility, and overall decision-making processes. This ties in to the covariances reflected in the model as barriers (challenges) and contingencies (facilitators) to the pursuit of innovation and productivity (see Figure 11). As the world moves forward, it should be recognized that future crises that impact organizations on either a local or global level can play a role in the overall ambidexterity process for leaders within the nonprofit sector. The nature of this impact requires further exploration.

Ambidexterity in the Nonprofit Space

As Peng (2019) noted, there is a lack of research specific to ambidexterity in the

nonprofit space. A key question in this research was to identify ambidextrous leadership

behaviors and the perception of their use specifically from the voice of nonprofit leaders. Peng's

review of existing literature and successive case study identified that there is value in the use of

ambidexterity in the nonprofit sector, particularly as organizations are called to maximize

resources and embrace tensions associated with capacity and organizational priority. These

themes were reinforced through analysis of the data collected within this study as well.

The framework presented by Peng (2019) focused on ambidexterity's role in supporting

public value creation, the use of different types of ambidexterity (structural, sequential, etc.)

based on the organizational need, and specifically mentioned the role of collaboration as a

functional factor in their framework. Peng also noted that tensions generated from the

collaborative process and an ambidextrous approach can play an important role in supporting this

expected tension. Results from this study serve to reinforce and extend the value and role of

collaboration (or joint space) within the nonprofit context. As nonprofit organizations prioritize

the maximizing of current resources, seeking opportunities to engage in collaboration are a

logical need. Collaboration and shared leadership are already identified within the research

literature as common vehicles for nonprofit optimization (Bryson et al., 2015; Freund, 2017;

Routhieaux, 2015; Tsasis, 2009); therefore, an expanded understanding of the role that

collaboration and shared leadership can play for nonprofit leaders within the context of an

ambidextrous approach adds new insight and dimension to the existing research base.

Further, Peng's model, based on a review of existing research and a single case study of

one French nonprofit, is structured as a dual circuit sequence. In contrast, analysis of data from this study reveals more of a cyclical aspect to the process. While more research is needed to understand this process with greater depth, the framework generated by analysis from this study provides a structure that aligns with and expands upon existing research to better understand the process nonprofit leaders use to simultaneously pursue the challenges of innovation and efficiency.

Reflection from participants around what makes the nonprofit space different from that of the for-profit world may support expansion of current research. For example, participant reflection on the combination of fear and discomfort with utilizing traditional business practices in the nonprofit space brings forward very important points also reflected in the literature (Aboraman & Kundi, 2020; Brimhall, 2021, Peng, 2019) . Perhaps the role of ambidexterity in nonprofit organizations is not as different as it is underexplored due to a combination of both awareness and understanding. This highlights the importance of this study and the need for continued exploration.

Breaking Down Silos

Berman (2016) postulated that silos are an inevitability in "any organization structure inhabited by human beings" (p. 75). A significant theme that emerged from multiple interviews was the role nonprofit leaders play in breaking down silos, particularly within the context of joint space. Silos are artificial or psychological barriers that form in many organizations or program structures. While they can be practical in terms of organizational efficiency, silos can lead to knowledge hoarding, an insular mindset, and overall program ineffectiveness (Waal et al., 2019). The role of leadership is to look for ways to break down the barriers that silos can reinforce and maximize opportunities for collaboration (Berman, 2016). P4 shared this concept in detail:

> We've got a new CEO and he's very different from the past CEO…and one of his
> qualities, I think that [has] been very helpful is his ability to collaborate…he's been
> working with the like [minded] initiatives or work groups.…And he's got a real good
> ability to kind of pull someone from three or four places where, in the past, the way has
> been to look for the expert, you know, and the expert might be involved in that [isolated
> group].

By capitalizing on opportunities for shared leadership within the organization, the CEO was able to bring people together. This maximized opportunities for both innovation and efficiency. As P4 said later, "I think people are starting to see [this style] works and people [were] used to being in, like, silos."

Other interviews reflected this need to "break down silos" through collaboration with external partners. P1 shared how individuals served by their social service nonprofit come to the organization with multiple needs.

> What we're seeing now and what really actually was always already in place, but like
> we're really becoming aware of it, is [that] we have individuals that are crossing so many
> multiple silos and you get your best outcomes when you provide services based on the
> whole individual. And you can't do that if you remain in your silos. So, it's really taking
> collaboration between our [program A] and [program B] and case managers, working
> with individuals in our state psychiatric hospitals. You know, individuals don't fit neatly
> [into boxes].…You know, recognizing that in order to provide successful services to
> individuals, we have to break down those silos and we have to collaborate with other
> partners.

The structure and design of a senior leadership team can support the idea of breaking down silos (Berman, 2016). The model proposed in this study endorses this by placing an emphasis on the function of joint space in the pursuit of innovation and productivity. The role of the senior leadership team should be to consciously break down silos by encouraging and facilitating cross-team thinking.

Waal et al. (2019) also examined which silo-busting techniques were most effective when utilized by leaders. An emphasis on continuous improvement, employee quality, and an orientation to long-term goals were identified as the most effective tactics. This was also supported by the model proposed in this study, particularly in the contingencies that facilitate ambidexterity and the overall learning or coaching mindset as a context for both innovation and production. A key question that leaders can ask when working within joint space is, "Does my work with others encourage collaboration that drives innovation or efficiency? If so, how?"

Recommendations

As with all studies, there are limitations to this research. It is difficult to know whether these findings are true across all nonprofit sectors. Also, all of the participants worked at nonprofits with budgets of $1 million or more. This excludes perspectives from many nonprofit organizations. The participants in the sample were also predominantly white and/or women. While this does reflect the current demographic makeup of nonprofit leadership in the United States (Buteau, 2019), it would be interesting to understand whether there are differences in leadership perspective or practice across gender and race or ethnicity. Also, while the initial aim of the study was to investigate leadership perspectives from nonprofit organizations in one geographic region of the United States (Richmond, Virginia); however, the geographic criteria was broadened and this may have limited the conclusions that could be drawn from a more

homogeneous geographic population.

Individuals leading organizations with much smaller budgets face significant capacity

challenges. These challenges are compounded in organizations that serve or are led by

individuals who are historically marginalized, such as people of color. It is particularly important

to note that this research does not reflect those perspectives and future research should seek to

include these voices for the purposes of equity.

Individuals leading organizations with much smaller budgets face significant capacity

challenges. These challenges are compounded in organizations that serve or are led by

individuals who are historically marginalized, such as people of color. It is particularly important

to note that this research does not reflect those perspectives and future research should seek to

include these voices for the purposes of equity.

Future research could explore these specific differences through quantitative research that

would look at different approaches to ambidexterity (and specifically use of ambidexterity within

joint space contexts) across differences in leader characteristics (gender and/or race/ethnicity) or

organizational characteristics (nonprofit size or nonprofit sector).

Additional research could explore the difference (or lack of difference) in perception

between innovation and production behaviors. This could be examined through either a

quantitative study or through further grounded theory research as an extension of this current

study.

A noted limitation within this study is that perspectives from the interview participants

came on the heels of the COVID-19 pandemic. Leader perceptions of crisis and reactions to

crisis were largely framed around this recent global event. Future research should keep this perspective in mind. As the imminent pressure of the early impact of COVID-19 on the workplace fades, leaders may shift their views regarding crisis or have additional perspectives based on new or different challenges that emerge within the workplace.

It is still difficult to determine whether there are significant differences in an ambidextrous approach between for-profit and nonprofit leaders. This could be an additional comparative study, controlling for organizational size and leader characteristics through quantitative research.

While this research revealed challenges unique to the nonprofit sector, it still explored larger organizations. Questions remain regarding specific challenges that face much smaller nonprofits with respect to their capacity, barriers to growth, and needs based on their organization's life cycle and development. A similarly structured qualitative study focused specifically on small nonprofits (with budgets under $1 million) could further explore some of the concepts that emerged from discussions with research participants in this study, including: (a) general perspectives on ambidexterity, innovation, and productivity for much smaller nonprofit organizations; (b) the adoption and perception of nonprofit versus for profit skills and strategies; and (c) the role of organizational resiliency with respect to innovation and ambidexterity.

Implications

As mentioned previously, ambidexterity and complexity within the nonprofit sector has not been studied with the same depth and rigor as organizations in for-profit contexts (Aboramadan & Kundi, 2020; Brimhall, 2021). This study adds new information to the body of research in nonprofit leadership, particularly in the areas of ambidexterity and complexity.

Utilizing the conceptual framework identified through this study, future research could explore development of a measurement tool that would allow nonprofit leaders to build awareness of their use of exploration and exploitation behaviors. Such a tool could help leaders identify how they currently manage their work within teams, both internally and externally. A measurement tool could look at leadership behaviors at both the individual level and the team level to support organizational strategic planning, individual professional development, and best practices in the use of joint space opportunities (collaboration and shared leadership).

An ideal tool would provide a baseline for the individual or team and also allow for ways to mark progress over time. A similar comparative tool would be the Competing Values Framework (Cameron & Quinn, 2011), which supports organizational planning with respect to structure and culture. The ambidexterity tool could examine time spent in innovation, production, and enabling leadership space. The prescriptive component of the tool would guide the leader on how to shift their time spent in each space over time within an organization as the leader aims for balance with respect to the organization's capacity needs.

The results of this study can also support nonprofit leaders in their ability to gain awareness around their own use of ambidexterity in their work. Both ambidexterity and complexity are relatively new concepts in the sphere of leadership development. Tools such as the conceptual framework identified within this study can help nonprofit leaders understand the role that balance plays in structuring their work. This can be used in either an individual coaching context or through strategic planning with the organization as a whole.

Finally, information gained through this study can support nonprofit leaders and an organization's board of directors in developing a culture that promotes an ambidextrous approach to management of the organization. It is important for nonprofit organizations to realize that leadership is not an *all or nothing* approach in terms of style. Leaders need to engender a combination of both vision and action in order to be successful. This should be seen as a dynamic process over time with frequent monitoring to understand the current needs for the organization as time passes.

Conclusion

This study aligns with and reinforces previous research on ambidexterity, particularly with how it is utilized by leaders in nonprofit organizations. The model proposed by this study expands on previous research by providing further detail on the stages involved in the pursuit of innovation or productivity. It also clarifies the barriers and contingencies that impact these processes from the perspective of nonprofit leaders. The balance between innovation and productivity is understood as a dynamic process that is facilitated through the use of joint space, either through collaboration (externally) or shared leadership (internally). This study provides an expanded understanding of the role that joint space plays in the work of nonprofit leaders due to both capacity challenges and the function of their work.

Future research should expand this inquiry across leader demographics, organization size, and organization type. Both quantitative and qualitative methods could offer expanded insights on the existence of these leadership behaviors and needs across populations. Particular attention should be paid to organizations with significantly smaller budgets (less than $500K) and leaders from historically marginalized demographic groups, such as people of color. Additional research could also support further exploration of the differences between the pursuit of productivity and innovation by nonprofit leaders.

The conclusions of this study can support existing research by adding new depth and understanding to the use of ambidexterity within the nonprofit sector. The conceptual framework created through this research can serve as the platform for a measurement tool that can support leader self-awareness of ambidextrous skills to support maximal outcomes for their teams and organizations. The framework also provides an expanded understanding of ambidexterity and its use within the nonprofit space, particularly when engaging in collaborative efforts with similarly minded organizations. Information gained from this study can be utilized by nonprofit leaders and their boards to support strategic planning, hiring considerations, and development of a culture that promotes an ambidextrous approach to leadership and organizational management.